CHICKEN COOKBOOK

PUBLISHER REPRESENTATIVE OFFICE

UNITED STATES: Prime Communication System
P.O.BOX456 Shaw Island, WA 98286

AUTHOR'S SALES AGENCY: A.K. HARANO COMPANY
P.O. Box 1022 Edmonds, WA 98020
Phone: (206) 774-5490
D & BH ENTERPRISES
94-443 Kahuanani Street, Waipahu, HI 96797
Phone: (808) 671-6041

OVERSEAS DISTRIBUTORS

UNITED STATES: JP TRADING, INC.
300 Industrial Way
Brisbane, Calif. 94005
Phone: (415) 468-0775, 0776

MEXICO: Publicaciones Sayrols, S.A. de C.V.

COLOMBIA: Jorge E. Morales & CIA. LTDA.

TAIWAN: Formosan Magazine Press, Ltd.

HONG KONG: Apollo Book Company, Ltd.

THAILAND: Central Department Store Ltd.

SINGAPORE: MPH DISTRIBUTORS (S) PTE, LTD.

MALAYSIA: MPH DISTRIBUTORS SDN, BHD.

PHILIPPINES: National Book Store, Inc.

KOREA: Tongjin Chulpan Muyeok Co., Ltd.

INDONESIA: C.V. TOKO BUKU "MENTENG"

INDIA: Dani Book Land, Bombay 14

AUSTRALIA: BOOKWISE INTERNATIONAL

GUAM, SIPAN AND MICRONESIAN ISLANDS: ISLAND PLANT-LIFE PRODUCTS

CANADA: MILESTONE PUBLICATIONS

U.S.A.: MASA T. & ASSOCIATES

ISBN4-915249-70-0

ACKNOWLEDGMENTS

I wish to express my heartfelt gratitude to many people for their invaluable assistance in the making of "CHICKEN COOKBOOK".

First my special thanks go to my publisher, Shiro Shimura, for his trust and faith in my work; to Akira Naito, who kindled my enthusiasm and got the project going.

Also to the following:
Photography: Kazuo Hara
Editorial Assistance: Sumiko Kobayashi, Atsuko Murata, Harue and Takeshi Harada
Illustration: Koh Minagawa, Michiko Hayashi
Design: Koji Abe, Mariko Suzuki, Tamami Chiba
Kitchen Help: Eiko Oishi

I am indebted to you all for your support, encouragement and patience during the many months of writing.

INTRODUCTION

Eight years ago I wrote my first cookbook, "Quick & Easy Tofu Cook Book". I was pleased, with its publication, to be able to bring to a reader the benefits of a diet which included frequent use of TOFU (soy bean cake), and its many different recipes. I was told by my mother, a most gifted cook, that good nutrition was a prime essential for mental and physical well being. I firmly believe that good nutrition, and plain common sense living are man's best medicine. Since my first "Tofu Cook Book" in 1982, I have written others which include "Sushi Cook Book", Japanese Cuisine For Everyone", "A Taste of Tofu", and other ethnic cookbooks.

Today there is a new generation of gourmets who have a deep appreciation of fine foods, and who take pride and pleasure in their preparation. There are in addition many more who have become more aware of the importance of good nutrition to health, as I do.

My interests in good nutrition include poultry, which is universally enjoyed, and widely available throughout the year. Poultry is higher in protein content, lower in calories and cholesterol, and is relatively inexpensive when compared to beef or pork. In addition it is well suited for microwave cooking.

With this new edition cookbook, I offer recipes from the Orient, where Japanese and Chinese are masters of the culinary art. Also included are recipes from the Western world, where evolved remarkable regional specialties.

Most of the contained recipes serve four persons. These amounts allow flexibility, and can be halved or doubled successfully. Most of the recipes take only a short time to prepare, and are easy to cook. Some of the necessary ingredients, however, may be unfamiliar to you. They are listed on page 108, and are available at most Oriental food markets, and at some health food stores and super markets.

It is my pleasure to share these recipes with you, the nutrition-conscious, and the gourmet cook...

January, 1990

Yukiko Moriyama

MAP OF JAPAN

Japan and its products

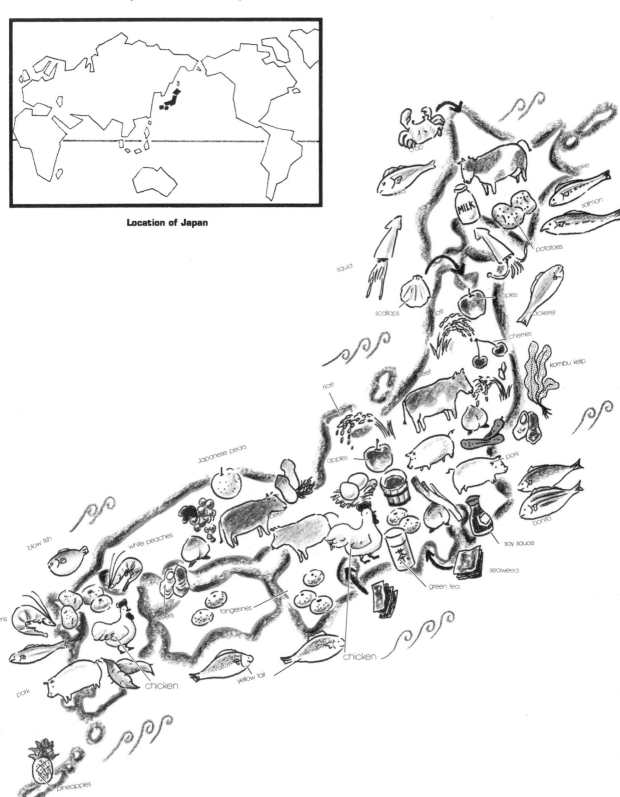

Location of Japan

5

CONTENTS

CONTENTS

BASIC COOKING INFORMATION

1 cup is equivalent to 240 ml in our recipes: (American cup measurement)

1 American cup = 240 ml = 8 American fl oz
1 British cup = 200 ml = 7 British fl oz
1 Japanese cup = 200 ml

1 tablespoon = 15 ml   1 teaspoon = 5 ml

ABBREVIATIONS USED IN THIS BOOK

C = cup (s)	T = tablespoon (s)	t = teaspoon (s)	fl = fluid	oz = ounce (s)
lb (s) = pound (s)	ml = milliliter	g = grams	in = inch (es)	cm = centimeter
F = Fahrenheit	C = Celsius	doz = dozen	pkg (s) = package (s)	
pt (s) = pint (s)	qt (s) = quart (s)			

TABLES CONVERTING FROM U.S. CUSTOMARY SYSTEM TO METRICS

Liquid Measures

U.S. Customary system	oz	g	ml
$1/16$ cup = 1 T	$1/2$ oz	14 g	15 ml
$1/4$ cup = 4 T	2 oz	60 g	59 ml
$1/2$ cup = 8 T	4 oz	115 g	118 ml
1 cup = 16 T	8 oz	225 g	236 ml
$1\,3/4$ cups	14 oz	400 g	414 ml
2 cups = 1 pint	16 oz	450 g	473 ml
3 cups	24 oz	685 g	710 ml
4 cups	32 oz	900 g	946 ml

Liquid Measures

Japanese system	oz	ml
$1/8$ cup	$7/8$ oz	25 ml
$1/4$ cup	$1\,3/4$ oz	50 ml
$1/2$ cup	$3\,1/2$ oz	100 ml
1 cup	7 oz	200 ml
$1\,1/2$ cups	$10\,1/2$ oz	300 ml
2 cups	14 oz	400 ml
3 cups	21 oz	600 ml
4 cups	28 oz	800 ml

Weights

ounces to grams*
$1/4$ oz = 7 g
$1/2$ oz = 14 g
1 oz = 30 g
2 oz = 60 g
4 oz = 115 g
6 oz = 170 g
8 oz = 225 g
16 oz = 450 g

*Equivalent

Linear Measures

inches to centimeters
$1/2$ in = 1.27 cm
1 in = 2.54 cm
2 in = 5.08 cm
4 in = 10.16 cm
5 in = 12.7 cm
10 in = 25.4 cm
15 in = 38.1 cm
20 in = 50.8 cm

Temperatures

Fahrenheit (F) to Celsius (C)		
freezer storage	−10°F =	−23.3°C
	0°F =	−17.7°C
water freezes	32°F =	0 °C
	68°F =	20 °C
	100°F =	37.7°C
water boils	212°F =	100 °C
	300°F =	148.8°C
	400°F =	204.4°C

Deep-Frying Oil Temperatures

300°F − 330°F (150°C − 165°C)	= low
340°F − 350°F (170°C − 175°C)	= moderate
350°F − 360°F (175°C − 180°C)	= high

Oven Temperatures

250°F − 350°F (120°C − 175°C)	= low or cool
350°F − 400°F (175°C − 204°C)	= moderate or medium
400°F − 450°F (204°C − 230°C)	= hot
450°F − 500°F (230°C − 260°C)	= very hot

INGREDIENTS

① GREEN ONION
② *DAIKON* RADISH
③ CELERY
④ CAULIFLOWER
⑤ CABBAGE
⑥ LETTUCE
⑦ BANANAS
⑧ PLAIN YOGURT
⑨ CREAM CHEESE
⑩ *YUZU* CITRON
⑪ GRAPEFRUIT
⑫ ZUCCHINI
⑬ CUCUMBER
⑭ ASPARAGUS
⑮ CARROT
⑯ PARSLEY
⑰ SPINACH
⑱ FRESH CREAM
⑲ BUTTER
⑳ SALMON
㉑ TOMATO
㉒ LEMON
㉓ KIWI FRUIT
㉔ ONION
㉕ FRESH MUSHROOM
㉖ BAMBOO SHOOT
㉗ CHEDDAR CHEESE
㉘ SWISS CHEESE
㉙ OYSTER

㉚ GARLIC
㉛ JAPANESE GREEN
  CHILI PEPPER
㉜ STRAWBERRIES
㉝ GREEN PEPPER
㉞ RADISH
㉟ RADISH SPROUTS
㊱ *SHIMEJI* MUSHROOM
㊲ GINGER ROOT
㊳ HORSERADISH MUSTARD
㊴ SLICED COOKED HAM
㊵ TINY SPROUTS
㊶ STEMS OF FLOWERING
  SEED PODS
㊷ *SHISO* LEAVES
㊸ CHINESE PICKLES
㊹ BEAN SPROUTS
㊺ SHRIMP
㊻ CHRYSANTHEMUM
㊼ *KINOME* SPRIG
㊽ *BENITADE*
㊾ GREEN PEAS
㊿ MIXED VEGETABLES
51 EGGS
52 GROUND MEAT
53 PORK SHOULDER LOIN
54 CHICKEN BREASTS
55 PORK SLICES
56 BEEF SLICES

FRESH FOODS

SEASONINGS

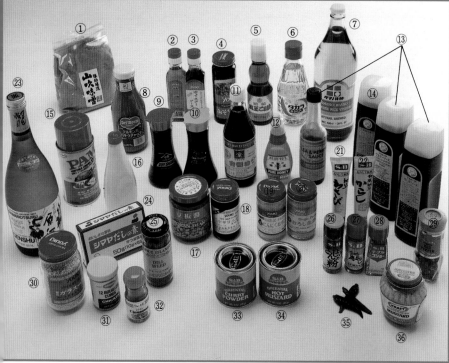

① *MISO*
② CHILI OIL
③ OYSTER SAUCE
④ SWEET BEAN SAUCE
⑤ SESAME SEED OIL
⑥ *MIRIN*
⑦ VINEGAR
⑧ KETCHUP
⑨ SOY SAUCE
⑩ LOW SALT SOY SAUCE
⑪ LIGHT SOY SAUCE
⑫ HONEY
⑬ WORCESTERSHIRE SAUCE
⑭ *TONKATSU* SAUSE
⑮ LOW-CALORIE COOKING OIL SPRAY
⑯ MAYONNAISE
⑰ HOT BEAN PASTE
⑱ SWEET BEAN PASTE
⑲ GRATED GARLIC
⑳ GRATED GINGER ROOT
㉑ *WASABI* PASTE
㉒ CHINESE MUSTARD PASTE
㉓ *SAKE*
㉔ *DASHI-NO-MOTO* (INSTANT SOUP MIX)
㉕ DILL WEED
㉖ *SANSHO* POWDER
㉗ 7-SPICE POWDER
㉘ PEPPER
㉙ CRUSHED RED PEPPER
㉚ CHICKEN SOUP STOCK
㉛ CHICKEN BOUILLON CUBES
㉜ CINNAMON
㉝ CURRY POWDER
㉞ MUSTARD POWDER
㉟ DRIED RED PEPPER
㊱ HORSERADISH MUSTARD

9

CHICKEN SALAD WITH ASPIC RING

A colorful dish which can be served at an elegant party.

INGREDIENTS: 4 to 6 servings

Chicken Salad:
14 ounces (400 grams) deboned and skinned chicken
    breast, cooked
$1/2$ cup chopped celery
$1/2$ cup shredded carrot
2 small green peppers, chopped
1 cup pineapple chunks, drained
$1/2$ cup mayonnaise
$1/4$ cup sour cream

1. Dice cooked chicken breast. Chop celery, green peppers, shred carrot and drain pineapple chunks.

2. Mix mayonnaise with sour cream.

3. Toss with chicken, celery, green peppers, carrot and pineapple chunks.

7 × 2-inch (18 × 5 cm) Aspic ring mold

2 tablespoons unflavored gelatine
4 tablespoons water
1½ cups chicken broth
1 cup tomato juice
Salt and pepper to taste
1 hard-boiled egg, sliced

1. Mix gelatine and 4 tablespoons water in a small sauce pan. Stir over low heat until mixture is hot. Heat chicken broth to lukewarm. Turn off heat and mix with tomato juice.

2. Pour gelatine mixture, chicken broth and tomato juice, salt and pepper into a glass bowl. Chill until slightly thickened and syrupy.

3. Place sliced egg into lightly oiled ring.

Note:
Potato or macaroni salad can be substituted for chicken salad.

4. Pour gelatine mixture in the ring. Chill until firm in a refrigerator.

5. Unmold by placing a serving platter on top of mold, then invert. Combine all salad ingredients; fill the center of the aspic.

Microwaved Chicken Breasts

2 large whole chicken breasts
1½ tablespoons *sake*

Note:
As a general rule, cooking chicken takes 6 minutes per pound in microwave oven on full power, HIGH(9).

1. Pierce the chicken breasts in a few places. Sprinkle *sake* and leave for 10 minutes. Place the breasts in microwave-safe dish, skin side down. Cover with plastic wrap.

2. Cook on HIGH(9) or on full power for 4 minutes; turn the chicken; cook for 1 minute longer. Chicken is cooked if a skewer comes out clean. Allow to cool.

JELLIED CHICKEN SALAD

A colorful salad dish that will add zest to a party menu.

INGREDIENTS: 4 to 6 servings

6 × 5¼ × 1¾-inch (15 × 13.5 × 4.5 cm) chicken Aspic mold

1 tablespoon unflavored gelatine
1²/₃ cups chicken broth
1 teaspoon light color soy sauce
2 cups diced cooked chicken
2 tablespoons lemon juice
¼ cup sliced cucumber
1 teaspoon salt
2 tablespoons pimiento-stuffed green olives

1 tablespoon minced green onion
½ teaspoon salt
⅛ teaspoon pepper

Garnishes:
Green pepper
Red pepper
Tomato
Lettuce

1. Soften gelatine in ½ cup cold broth. Heat and stir over low heat until gelatine dissolves. Stir in remaining broth. Add 1 teaspoon soy sauce. Chill until partially set.

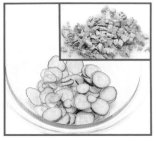

2. Slice cucumber and sprinkle 1 teaspoon salt to soften cucumber slices. Drain liquid.

3. Mix remaining ingredients. Fold into gelatine; pour into jelly roll pan. Chill until set. Unmold on plate. Garnish with lettuce, sliced peppers and tomato wedges.

STUFFED TOMATOES

Stuffed tomatoes make a sumptuous low-calorie side dish with almost any entrée, or to serve as a light lunch dish.

INGREDIENTS: 4 servings

4 firm tomatoes
1/3 cup cooked diced chicken breast
1/3 cup diced celery
1/4 cup mayonnaise
1 teaspoon lemon juice
Salt and pepper to taste
Pinch of paprika
2 pimiento-stuffed green olives, sliced

1. Cut the top off the tomatoes.

2. Scoop out the flesh and seeds. Use pulp for another purpose. Sprinkle lemon juice. Turn upside down to drain briefly.

3. Toss chicken, celery, lemon juice, salt and pepper together.

4. Mix in mayonnaise. Spoon the chicken into the tomatoes. Sprinkle paprika. Garnish with sliced olives.

CHICKEN-AND-CABBAGE SALAD

Coleslaw will never seem the same with sour cream dressing.

INGREDIENTS: 4 servings

3 cups shredded cabbage (about $^1/_2$ medium head)
1 small carrot, shredded
$^1/_4$ cup raisins
4 ounces (115 grams) cooked chicken, deboned and skinned

Salad Dressing: Makes $^2/_3$ cup
$^1/_2$ cup sour cream
2 tablespoons rice vinegar
$^1/_4$ teaspoon salt
1 teaspoon salt
1 teaspoon sugar
$^1/_2$ teaspoon dry mustard
Dash of freshly ground pepper
$^1/_4$ teaspoon light-color soy sauce
Paprika, if desired

1. Shred the cabbage, using a large sharp knife. Shred carrot. Slice cooked chicken into julienne strips.

2. Mix all salad dressing ingredients. Beat until smooth.

3. Combine cabbage, carrot, raisins and chicken. Toss with dressing.

CURRY FLAVORED CHICKEN SALAD

Curry powder and ketchup add a tantalizing color and enhance the flavor of French dressing.

INGREDIENTS: 4 servings

4 ounces (115 grams) cooked chicken meat
1 block (14 to 16 ounces, 400 to 450 grams) firm *tofu*, well drained
1 green pepper
1 Japanese cucumber
Some lettuce leaves
Salad Dressing:
2 teaspoons curry powder
1/2 cup French dressing

1 tablespoon grated onion
1 tablespoon ketchup
Pinch of ground cumin
Dash of white pepper

Note:
To drain tofu, wrap in paper towel and place on a bamboo tray or slanted board next to sink, for about an hour.

1. Boil *tofu* in hot water for 2 minutes. Drain and chill.

2. Cut into bite size pieces. Cut cooked chicken meat into serving sizes.

3. Make salad dressing. Mix all ingredients. Divide into two equal portions.

4. Marinate *tofu* and chicken in dressing. Chill for one hour. Slice cucumber and green pepper; mix with chicken. Mix chicken with *tofu*. Toss lightly. Serve it with lettuce.

SPICY CUCUMBER-AND-CHICKEN SALAD

If planning a low-calorie meal, try this spicy but healthful dish.

INGREDIENTS: 4 servings

2 large whole chicken breasts
2 to 3 Japanese cucumbers or zucchini

Tofu Mayonnaise for Chicken:
Makes ³/₄ cup
7 ounces (200 grams) *tofu*, well drained
7 tablespoons vegetable oil
3 tablespoons rice vinegar
2 tablespoons lemon juice

2 heaping teaspoons red *miso**
1 teaspoon salt
¹/₈ teaspoon pepper

Hot Bean Sauce for Cucumbers:
¹/₂ teaspoon Chinese hot bean paste*
²/₃ teaspoon salt
1 teaspoon sesame oil*
1 tablespoon toasted sesame seeds

*Available at Oriental stores.

1. Combine all *tofu* mayonnaise ingredients in a blender; beat until smooth, 30 seconds. Cook chicken breasts. (See page 11)

2. Cut cooked chicken into julienne strips; toss lightly with *tofu* mayonnaise. Chill in a refrigerator.

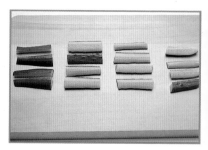

3. Cut cucumbers into halves lengthwise. Cut each piece into fourths crosswise. Mix hot bean paste, salt and sesame oil; toss with cucumbers. Mix chilled chicken breasts and cucumbers. Sprinkle sesame seeds on top.

CHICKEN-VEGETABLE MEDLEY

Zucchini can be substituted for Japanese cucumbers.

INGREDIENTS: 4 servings

4 ounces (115 grams) cooked chicken breast, deboned and skinned
12 ounces (340 grams) beansprouts
1 Japanese cucumber
1 tomato
1/2 teaspoon grated lemon peel

Dressing: Japanese Style:
2 tablespoons rice vinegar
2 tablespoons soy sauce
1 teaspoon sugar
1/4 teaspoon sesame oil
1 teaspoon hot mustard

Garnishes:
Chopped fresh coriander leaves
Toasted sesame seeds

Note: Dressing: Thai Style
1/2 teaspoon finely chopped garlic
1/2 teaspoon red pepper flakes
1/2 teaspoon freshly ground pepper
Lime, squeezed
1 teaspoon sugar
1 cup mayonnaise
1 tablespoon fish oil*

*Available at Oriental stores.

1. Shred or slice chicken breast into julienne strips; mix with grated lemon peel.

2. In teflon-coated skillet, stir fry beansprouts lightly over medium heat without oil until soft. Allow to cool.

3. Slice cucumber thinly. Cut tomato into wedges. Combine chicken, beansprouts and cucumber slices; toss lightly with dressing. Arrange tomato wedges.

SWEET AND SOUR CUCUMBER-AND-CHICKEN SALAD

This delicate salad dressing is a great favorite in Japan.

INGREDIENTS: 4 servings

1 whole chicken breast, deboned and skinned
1¹/₂ cups water
2 tablespoons *sake*

4 small Japanese cucumbers
1 teaspoon salt

Sweet And Sour Salad Dressing:
5 tablespoons Japanese rice vinegar
2 tablespoons soy sauce
1 tablespoon *mirin*, Japanese sweet cooking wine
1 tablespoon sugar

1. Place chicken breast in skillet, pour water and *sake* over it. Cover with lid and bring to a boil over medium heat. Lower the heat and cook until most of liquid is gone. Allow to cool. Slice into julienne strips. Chill in the refrigerator.

2. Slice cucumbers thinly; sprinkle salt. Leave for 10 minutes. Squeeze out excess water. Mix chicken and cucumbers; toss with salad dressing.

18

SPINACH SALAD WITH SESAME SEEDS

Sesame seeds bring a rich nutty flavor to this spinach salad.

INGREDIENTS: 4 servings

4 ounces (115 grams) deboned and skinned cooked
   chicken breast (see page 11)
1 bunch fresh spinach

Salad Dressing:
3 tablespoons toasted white sesame seeds
2²/₃ tablespoons chicken broth
1 tablespoon light-color soy sauce
¹/₂ teaspoon sugar

1. Cut boneless chicken breast into julienne strips.

2. Parboil spinach in lightly salted water until just tender; rinse in cold water to retain color. Gently squeeze out water. Cut off stem ends; cut into 1¹/₂-inch (4 cm) lengths.

3. Grind sesame seeds in a mortar; add chicken broth, soy sauce and sugar. Mix chicken and spinach together. Add the mixture to dressing; toss lightly.

PITA BREAD (POCKET BREAD)

INGREDIENTS: Makes 4 breads

2 large Pita (pocket breads)
Fillings:
1½ cups cooked deboned chicken, diced
2 hard boiled eggs, chopped
4 tablespoons minced celery
1 tablespoon minced parsley
½ cucumber, chopped

Ⓐ
- ¼ cup mayonnaise
- ¼ teaspoon curry powder
- ½ teaspoon ground coriander or white *miso*

4 black or pimiento-stuffed olives

Filled with meat or salad, it is delicious for lunch or light supper.

1. Fillings.

2. For chopped egg, slice hard-boiled egg as shown.

3. Slice egg vertically.

4. Combine all ingredients Ⓐ; mix with filling. Divide into fourths.

5. Cut Pita in half. Fill with the filling. Top with an olive.

BREAKFAST PIE, COUNTRY OMELET

CUT STYLE

A bright touch of color and a savory flavor of chicken will be particularly prized for Sunday brunch.

INGREDIENTS: 4 servings

4 to 5 ounces (115 to 140 grams) chicken breast, deboned and skinned and cut into 1/2-inch cubes
1 tablespoon butter or margarine
1 teaspoon olive oil
2 medium potatoes, peeled and cut into 1/2-inch cubes
1 tablespoon minced parsley
1 tablespoon minced green onion
6 slightly beaten eggs
Salt and pepper to taste
1 tablespoon butter or margarine

Garnishes: Lemon
Parsley
Condiment: Ketchup

1. Fillings. Beat eggs lightly and season with salt and pepper; add parsley and green onion. Mix chicken pieces and eggs.

2. In a skillet, melt butter over medium heat; add chicken pieces. Stir-fry until color changes, about 3 minutes. Set aside.

3. Pour 1 teaspoon olive oil in skillet; add potatoes and cook over medium heat until golden.

4. Pour into skillet. Toss quickly with potato, shaking the skillet a few times to prevent sticking. Cook over medium heat, covered about 7 minutes. Add 1 tablespoon butter or margarine on the edge of the omelet, tilting skillet to let butter or margarine flow around it. If you prefer, place skillet under broiler to brown the top.

CHICKEN-POTATO *MISO* SOUP

Miso or soybean paste is one of the common ingredients of Japanese cooking.

INGREDIENTS: 4 servings

3¼ cups water
6 to 7 ounces (170 to 200 grams) cut-up chicken
2 small potatoes (8 ounces, 225 grams)
2 medium onions, cut into wedges
8 green beans (2 ounces, 60 grams)
3½ level tablespoons white *miso** (2½ ounces, 80 grams)

*Available at Oriental stores.

1. Peel potato, cut into bite size pieces. Cut onion into wedges. Snap ends off from beans and remove string. Boil in salted water until tender. Cut into 2-inch (5 cm) diagonal slices.

2. Cut chicken into 1½-inch (4 cm) pieces. In a 2-quart sauce pan, place chicken pieces and 3¼ cups water and cook over medium heat for 10 minutes. Skim froth.

3. Add potatoes and onions; cook until tender. Mix 4 tablespoons cooking broth with *miso* paste; add to the pot. Turn off heat just before boiling point. Add cooked green beans.

22

WHOLE CHICKEN SOUP

For a plain but healthful supper, serve this chicken soup with your favorite salad.

INGREDIENTS: 4 to 6 servings

$2^1/_2$ to $3^1/_4$ pounds ($1^1/_4$ to 2 kg) chicken
$6^1/_2$ cups hot water
$^1/_2$ leek, cut into 2 to 3 pieces
1-inch (2.5 cm) square ginger root, sliced
1 dried *shiitake* mushroom
1 tablespoon *sake*
$2^1/_2$ teaspoons salt
$^1/_2$ teaspoon light-color soy sauce
Dash of pepper

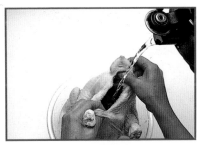

1. Wash and clean chicken; place the chicken in a pot and cover with water. Bring to a full boil.

2. Remove chicken and wash under running water. Place the chicken, leek, ginger root, *shiitake* mushroom in hot water; cook, covered for 1 to $1^1/_2$ hours over low heat. Skim froth and fat during cooking.

3. Season with salt, *sake* and soy sauce. Place the chicken carefully in a large serving bowl and pour over soup.

HEARTY CHICKEN HOT-POT

2¹/₂ to 3 pounds (1 to 1.5 kg) cut-up fryer chicken
4-inch-square (10 cm) *kombu* kelp*
1 bunch green onion
1 bunch spinach
¹/₃ cup *sake**
9¹/₂ to 10 cups water
Some Chinese cabbage (*Nappa* cabbage)

Dipping Sauce:
Makes 1¹/₂ cups
¹/₂ cup rice vinegar*
¹/₂ cup lemon juice
¹/₂ cup light-color soy sauce
Salt and pepper to taste

*Available at Oriental stores

This Oriental "fondue" is for an intimate dinner. Each person takes what he wants from the hot pot into his bowl.

1. Cut chicken into small serving pieces; place chicken in boiling water for 1 minute. Drain on a bamboo tray or colander.

2. Wipe *Kombu* kelp dry with paper towel. Cut green onion and spinach into 2-inch (5 cm) long pieces.

3. In a large earthenware or casserole dish, place kelp and then chicken pieces. Fill the pot with water and bring to a boil. Take out kelp and skim froth. Add *sake* and vegetables of your choice and cook over medium heat uncovered until chicken is ready to eat and vegetables are tender. Dip into sauce. Add more chicken pieces, vegetables and water to casserole as needed.

Condiment

How to Make *Momiji oroshi*

Grated *Daikon* radish
4 red chili pepper

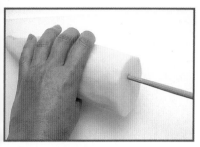

1. Peel washed dried *daikon* radish; make 3 to 4 holes in one end of radish with a pointed chopstick.

2. Cut stem end off dried chili peppers and remove seeds. Plug seeded chili peppers into the *daikon* radish holes, using a chopstick to push them.

3. Grate them together so that the radish is flecked with red.

BASIC CHICKEN STOCK

After the broth is cooked, reserve chicken for other uses.

1 stewing chicken, about 3¹/₂ pounds (1 to 1¹/₂ kg.)
Water to cook chicken
1¹/₂ teaspoons salt
1-inch (2.5 cm) square cube ginger root

1 scallion
1 stalk celery with leaves or 1 dried *shiitake* mushroom
Parsley (optional)
Light-color soy sauce to taste (optional)

1. Place stewing chicken, water and remaining ingredients to a pot and bring to a full boil, covered.

2. Turn heat to low and continue to cook simmering for 2 hours; skim froth and fat. Remove chicken. Allow chicken to cool. Strain soup stock with kitchen cloth or cheese cloth. Allow to cool, then refrigerate.

3. Remove fat with a strainer. Use the stock as needed.

Note:
A whole chicken makes 3 cups cooked boneless chicken meat.

How to store soup stock

Stock may be stored in the refrigerator for up to 5 days. Freeze stock in ice cube trays, then store in plastic bags for later use.

CHICKEN *SHABU-SHABU*

Thin slices of chicken are swished back and forth, and simmered in stock.

INGREDIENTS: 4 to 6 servings

Cooking Broth: Makes about 4 cups
2 whole chicken bones
4 to 5 cups warm water
Assorted vegetables (carrot, celery
  leaves, parsley, onion)

14 ounces (400 grams) chicken thigh,
  or chicken breasts
4 ounces (115 grams) chrysanthemum leaves, or spinach leaves
3½ ounces (100 grams) *shiitake*
  mushrooms

20 ounces (570 grams) yam noodles
  (*shirataki* filaments)

Dipping Sauce:
3 tablespoons white *miso*, soy bean
  paste.*
2 tablespoons *mirin*, Japanese sweet
  cooking wine*
2 tablespoons chicken stock

Condiment:
Chopped chives or scallion

*Available at Oriental stores.

BASIC SOUP STOCK

1. Clean chicken bones under running water; cut into large pieces.

2. Place bones, warm water and vegetable pieces in a pot and cook, over low heat uncovered for 1 to 2 hours. Skim froth and fat. Add water if necessary during cooking.

3. Strain soup stock with a fine mesh strainer lined with paper towel or cheese cloth.

4. Skim soup of excess fat with rice paper or allow to cool, then refrigerate. Fat will harden on the surface. Remove with a strainer.

PREPARATION

1. Remove bones and peel off skin from chicken flesh. Slice the flesh as thin as possible.

2. Blanch the skin in boiling water and turn into cold water. This makes the skin tender and crunchy, and also removes the odor.

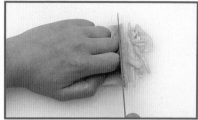

3. Cut the layers of skin into ¼-inch (7 mm) wide strips.

4. Trim away hard stems from chrysanthemum leaves. Cut into 2-inch (5 cm) length.

5. Trim off hard stem ends of mushrooms; make a decorative cut on the caps.

6. Wash and drain yam noodles.

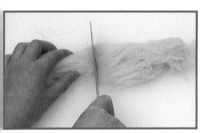

7. Cut into 3-inch (8 cm) length.

8. Arrange chicken, and other ingredients attractively on a plate.

9. Bring the stock to a boil in the pot; add yam noodles, mushrooms and chicken slices.

10. When chicken changes color, add chrysanthemum leaves.

11. Pour dipping sauce and condiment in each bowl and dip cooked food.

12. To make dipping sauce, cook dipping sauce ingredients in a small saucepan over low heat until thickened. Allow to cool, then transfer to a small bowl.

WINTER MELON SOUP

Slow simmering of the winter melon develops an irresistibly hearty homemade flavor.

INGREDIENTS: 4 to 6 servings

1¼ pounds (570 grams) chicken wings, or cut-up
   chicken
1½ pounds (685 grams) winter melon
1 green onion
½-inch (1.5 cm) thick ginger root, sliced or crushed
6½ cups water
2 teaspoons salt
1 tablespoon *sake*

1. Cut chicken wings in half; wash and pat dry with paper towels. If using cut-up chicken, cut into small serving pieces. Peel hard outer skin and remove seeds from melon; dice into 1⅛-inch (3 cm) cubes.

2. In a 3-quart pot, place chicken, scallion, ginger root and 6½ cups water; bring to a full boil; lower heat, and cook about 1 hour. Skim froth and fat.

3. Add diced winter melon and cook over medium heat until melon is cooked. Add salt and *sake* to taste.

CHICKEN-BALL SOUP

This is a variation of the Steamed Ground Chicken with Mixed Vegetables. (Page 48)

INGREDIENTS: 4 servings

1 stalk celery
10 ounces (285 grams) finely ground chicken breast

Ⓐ
- 1½ teaspoons grated ginger root
- 1 teaspoon salt
- ½ tablespoons *sake*
- 4 teaspoons cornstarch
- 2 egg whites, slightly beaten
- 2 teaspoons soy sauce
- ⅛ teaspoon vegetable oil
- ½ cups cooked mixed vegetables

2½ cups water
1 teaspoon light-color soy sauce
½ teaspoon salt
1 slice lemon, cut into fourths
(optional)

1. Cut celery into ½-inch (1.5 cm) long pieces.

2. Combine ground meat with ingredients Ⓐ. In 2-quart pan, pour 2½ cups water; bring to a boil.

3. Drop one spoonful of meat mixture, shaped into balls, into boiling water. Cook over medium heat; skim froth. Add celery; cook over medium heat until celery is tender. Season with soy sauce and salt.

CHICKEN *SUKIYAKI*

The enchanting combination of chicken and assorted vegetables serves as a smart party-brightener.

INGREDIENTS: 4 to 6 servings

2¹/₂ to 3 pounds (1¹/₄ to 1¹/₃ kg) cut-up chicken broiler-fryer or chicken breasts

2 blocks (14 to 16 ounces, 400 to 450 grams each) firm *tofu*

2 leeks

1 onion

14 ounces (400 grams) yam noodles*

1 bunch broccoli

1 tablespoon vegetable oil (optional)

Cooking Broth: Makes 3 cups

¹/₂ cup *mirin* (Japanese sweet cooking wine*)

¹/₂ cup sugar

¹/₂ cup soy sauce

2 cups chicken stock

*Available at Oriental stores.

1. Pour all cooking broth ingredients in a sauce pan and cook over medium heat until sugar dissolves. Set aside. Remove large leaves and cut off the woody stalk ends from broccoli. Steam until tender. Cut into 2-inch (5 cm) by ¹/₂-inch (1.5 cm) pieces. Slice leeks into 2-inch (5 cm) diagonal pieces.

2. Cut *tofu* into 1-inch (2.5 cm) cubes. Cut yam noodles for easy handling. Cut onion into halves and slice into half rings. Cut chicken into serving pieces. Arrange all ingredients on a large platter. Arrange small portion of each ingredient in a *Sukiyaki* pot. Pour ¹/₂ portion of cooking broth.

3. Cook the ingredients until the broth becomes bubbly or chicken pieces are cooked. Everyone can help themselves to their favorite ingredients. Continue cooking by adding small portion of ingredients, adding more broth as needed.

Chicken Bowl: 4 servings

3 to 4 cups hot steamed rice
4 eggs, lightly beaten

1. Heat leftover *Sukiyaki* and pour over beaten eggs evenly.
2. When eggs are almost set, turn off the heat.
3. In each serving bowl, place cooked rice. Pour egg mixture over rice.

A charming one bowl, dish omelet on rice is made with chicken and egg.

Microwaved Chicken Bowl

INGREDIENTS: 1 serving

1 to 1¼ cups cooked rice (see page 100)
4 to 5 ounces (130 grams) chicken breast, deboned and skinned
¼ medium onion, thinly sliced
1 egg, lightly beaten
Some *mitsuba* (trefoil) (optional)

Cooking Broth:

¼ cup soup stock
1½ teaspoons sugar
1 tablespoon *mirin* (Japanese sweet cooking wine)
1 tablespoon soy sauce

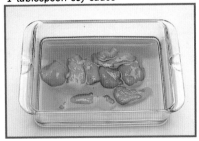

1. Cut chicken into bite size pieces. In a small microwave oven-proof dish, place chicken pieces. Pour cooking broth over. Cook on HIGH(9) for 3 minutes, covered.

2. Add sliced onion on top; cook on HIGH(9) for 3 more minutes.

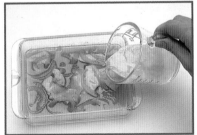

3. Pour over beaten egg; cook on HIGH(9) for 30 seconds. Let stand for 1 minute, covered. Place over hot cooked rice.

31

GRILLED *TOFU* WITH CHICKEN WINGS

This easy high-protein dish can be served with hot cooked rice.

INGREDIENTS: 4 servings

14 ounces (400 grams) firm *tofu*, well drained
3 tablespoons vegetable oil
14 ounces (400 grams) chicken wings
1 teaspoon chopped ginger root
Cooking Broth:
1¼ cups chicken broth
3 tablespoons soy sauce
3 tablespoons sugar
2 tablespoons *mirin*, Japanese sweet cooking wine*
1 tablespoon *sake*

*Available at Oriental stores

1. Heat 1 tablespoon oil in skillet; grill *tofu* on both sides until browned.

2. Cut into 1-inch (2.5 cm) cubes; set aside.

3. Add 2 tablespoons oil to the skillet and heat over medium heat; add chopped ginger root. Stir-fry for a minute; add wings and stir-fry until golden brown.

4. In 2-quart sauce pan, heat cooking broth until it comes to a boil; add wings and bring to a boil. Add *tofu* and cook covered over medium heat until most broth is absorbed.

32

The vegetables are cooked twice and flavored with salt, sugar and *sake.*

INGREDIENTS: 4 servings

³/₄ cup chicken stock
7 ounces (200 grams) *daikon* radish
1 medium carrot
2¹/₂ cups water or chicken stock
2¹/₂ ounces (70 grams) bamboo shoots
2 dried *shiitake* mushrooms, softened
8 ounces (225 grams) broccoli flowerets

1 can (4 ounces) button mushrooms, drained
4 water chestnuts
¹/₂ dried red chili pepper, minced
1 tablespoon vegetable oil
1 teaspoon salt
¹/₂ teaspoon sugar
1 tablespoon *sake*
1 teaspoon cornstarch plus 1 table-spoon water for thickening

1. Peel *daikon* radish and carrot with vegetable peeler. Cut *daikon* and bamboo shoots into ³/₄-inch (2cm) thick round, slices, and cut then into quarters. Slice carrot into ¹/₄-inch (7mm) thick round slices.

2. Soften *shiitake* mushrooms in water; trim off hard stem ends. Slice thin. Steam-cook broccoli flowerets. Cook *daikon* and carrot in 2¹/₂ cups water or chicken stock until tender. Save liquid.

3. In a wok, heat 1 tablespoon oil, stir-fry minced chili pepper; add bamboo shoots, mushrooms over medium heat for 2 to 3 minutes.

4. Pour 1 cup stock and bring to a boil. Add *daikon* and carrot. Thicken with cornstarch mixture. Add cooked broccoli flowerts; mix well.

33

CHICKEN WITH SQUASH

Chicken dish, mildly seasoned with broth, can be served hot or cold.

INGREDIENTS: 4 servings

1 large acorn squash or 21 ounces (600 grams) *kabocha* pumpkin
1 pound broiler-fryer or chicken wings or legs

3 to 4 cups water
1 tablespoon *sake**
1-inch (2.5 cm) cube ginger root, sliced

Cooking Broth:
3 tablespoons sugar
¹/₄ cup soy sauce
¹/₄ cup *mirin*, sweet Japanese cooking wine*

*Available at Oriental stores

1. Cook chicken with water, *sake* and sliced ginger root. Skim froth during cooking.

2. Cut squash into serving pieces; boil in salted water using medium heat until pulp is tender about 10 minutes.

3. Add squash to chicken. Pour cooking sauce. Cook combined ingredients over medium heat until half the liquid is reduced.

Note:
How to cook the acorn squash in a microwave oven:
1. Pierce the whole squash in several places with an ice pick or skewer.
2. Place on a paper towel. Cook on HIGH(9) for 4 minutes.
3. Turn the squash over; cook 4 minutes.
4. Cut the squash in half and remove the seeds and stringly fibers.

34

STUFFED CABBAGE

Stuffed vegetables are popular throughout the world. This recipe is popular among Japanese.

INGREDIENTS: Makes 4 rolls

12 to 16 ounces (340 to 450 grams) firm *tofu*, well drained
1 teaspoon salt
4 large Chinese cabbage leaves (Nappa)
1 whole chicken breast
1/2 cup chopped spinach leaves
1 teaspoon soy sauce
1 teaspoon *sake* or cooking wine

Cooking Broth:

1 1/2 cups chicken broth or 1 1/2 cups water plus 1 1/2 cubes of chicken bouillon
2 tablespoons *mirin* (Japanese sweet cooking rice wine)
1/8 teaspoon salt
Dash of pepper
1/2 tablespoon cornstarch, dissolved in 1/4 cup of water
1 carrot, cooked, as garnish

1. Crumble well drained *tofu* with potato masher; add salt and mix well.

2. Cook cabbage in boiling water until tender; drain. Remove bones and skin from chicken breast. Chop into small pieces.

3. Combine chicken, soy sauce and *sake* in a glass bowl. Mix *tofu*, chicken and chopped spinach leaves; and divide into four equal portions.

4. Place one part *tofu* mixture at stem end of each cabbage leaf. Roll leaf around *tofu* mixture, tucking in sides. Secure ends with toothpicks. Place rolls in a sauce pan, seam side down. Add chicken broth and cook for 15 minutes over medium heat. Add cornstarch mixture, stirring until thickened. Remove toothpicks. Serve garnished with cooked carrot.

35

CHICKEN AND VEGETABLE STEW

INGREDIENTS: 6 to 8 servings

1 pound (450 grams) fryer chicken, cut-up
1 tablespoon lemon juice
2 small (or 3 ~ 5) Japanese eggplants
2 small potatoes
2 tomatoes
1 onion
1 clove garlic, sliced
3 large slices ginger root
7 tablespoons vegetable oil
Ⓐ ⎰ 6 tablespoons soy sauce
   ⎱ 1 teaspoon sugar
      ³/₄ cup water
      1 teaspoon hot bean paste (chili paste with soybeans)*

*Available at Oriental stores

This colorful stew can be served as a light supper with your favorite bread or rice.

1. Cut chicken into 1¹/₂-inch (4 cm) pieces. Sprinkle lemon juice.

2. Cut eggplants into bite size pieces; soak in water. Peel potatoes and cut into small chunks. Boil potatoes until tender.

3. Cut tomatoes and onion into wedges.

4. Mix ingredients Ⓐ. Heat wok and add 3 tablespoons oil. Stir-fry eggplants over high heat for a minute. Remove eggplants from wok and set aside.

5. Pour remaining oil in wok; add garlic and ginger root and stir-fry over medium heat until aroma is released. Add chicken pieces and stir-fry for 7 minutes. Add onion and stir-fry until onion is soft. Add potato, tomatoes and ingredients Ⓐ; mix well and stir-fry for 5 more minutes. Pour all stir-fried ingredients into 2-quart casserole pot. Cook for 15 minutes over low heat. Add eggplants.

SWEET AND SOUR CHICKEN

INGREDIENTS: 4 servings

1½ pounds (685 grams) chicken breast or thighs
1 clove garlic, crushed
1 tablespoon vegetable oil
Sweet And Sour Sauce:
2 tablespoons soy sauce
⅔ cup water
3 tablespoons rice vinegar*
½ cup sugar
2 tablespoons cornstarch
1 tomato, cut into wedges
2 green peppers, cut into strips
2 slices pineapple, cut into eighths
Some roasted peanuts or sesame seeds

*Available at Oriental stores

The enchanting flavor of Sweet And Sour Sauce adds a novel taste to the most routine chicken dish.

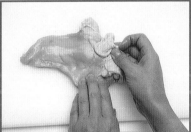

1. Peel off skin from chicken.

2. Cut into bite size pieces.

3. Heat a wok and add 1 tablespoon oil over medium heat. Stir-fry garlic until aroma is released.

4. Add chicken and stir-fry until golden brown. Drain excess grease from chicken.

5. In a 3-quart sauce pan, heat the Sweet And Sour Sauce ingredients over medium heat; stir until thickened.

6. Add tomato, green peppers and pineapple. Cook for 15 minutes, covered over medium heat. Serve with roasted peanuts or sesame seeds sprinkled on top.

CHICKEN CURRY

Serve this mild curry dish with hot rice or noodles.

INGREDIENTS: 4 servings

2¹/₂ to 3 pounds (1¹/₄ to 1¹/₃ kg) broiler-fryer chicken

Ⓐ ⎰ 3 cups water
   ⎱ 1 clove garlic, sliced
   ⎱ 1 teaspoon grated ginger root

1 cup coarsely chopped onion
1 carrot
1 stalk celery
1¹/₂ tablespoons curry powder
¹/₄ cup butter or margarine (¹/₈ pound-30 grams stick)

¹/₂ cup all-purpose flour
Some salt
Some sugar
1 cup milk
1 teaspoon lemon juice
¹/₂ apple, grated
¹/₂ cup seedless raisins

1. Cook chicken in ingredients Ⓐ until tender.

2. Discard bones and skin from chicken; cut into 1-inch (2.5 cm) pieces. Skim froth from the stock. Strain with cheese cloth or paper towel. Cut carrot into chunks. Cut celery into 1-inch (2.5 cm) thick slices.

3. Cook carrot and celery in salted water until tender. Melt butter or margarine in a skillet, sauté onion until tender.

4. Add curry powder.

5. Stir well and add salt, sugar and flour; mix well.

6. Pour 2 cups chicken stock slowly, stirring with wire whisk over low heat.

7. Add milk, stirring constantly.

8. Add chicken and vegetables.

9. Add lemon juice, grated apple, and raisins. Serve with hot cooked rice.

Curry Powder

Curry powder has long been known to Southeast Asia and Latin America. The bright yellow color and distinctive flavor come from a blend of many spices and herbs. It comes from India, although it is rarely used there. Usually it is made from scratch and each family blends its own according to personal taste.

Today, many commercial spice blends are sold at food shops and selecting what kind is a matter of personal taste.

About Rice

Rice has a long history as far back as 4000–3500 B.C. Biologically, there are two species. One is called ORYZA SATIVA which is grown in Asian countries and the other is called ORYZA GLABERRIMA which is cultivated in Africa. Both species were cultivated in India in the begining.

Today, many area of the world use rice and each country has developed its own rice recipes. Japanese rice is short-grain rice. In the U.S., short grain rice is grown extensively in California. Other types are long-grain rice and round-grain rice and rice cultivation techniques spread to many areas of the world.

A side serving of steamed or boiled rice provides accompaniment to many oriental dishes. Left-over cooked rice often can be used for fried rice. (See page 89 for the recipe).

This main dish recipe uses short-grain rice which is somewhat stickier and moister than long-grain rice. The fluffy and sticky textured rice is easier to hold with chopsticks.

GROUND CHICKEN MEAT STROGANOFF

1/2 cup minced onion
1 clove garlic, minced
2 tablespoons vegetable oil
1 pound (450 grams) ground or chopped chicken breast
2 tablespoons flour
1/2 teaspoon salt
1 teaspoon light-color soy sauce
1/4 teaspoon pepper
1 can (8 ounces, 225 grams) sliced mushrooms, drained
1 can (10 1/2 ounces, 300 grams) cream of chicken soup, undiluted
1 cup sour cream
1 tablespoon minced parsley

This pleasant and easy dish is sure to be one of your favorites for everyday dinner or party.

1. In a skillet, sauté onion and garlic in oil over medium heat until onion softens.

2. Add chopped or ground chicken meat; cook for 5 minutes over medium heat or until done.

Note:

Serve with hot cooked rice or Sesame Seed Noodles (Below).

Sesame Seed Noodles

INGREDIENTS: 4 servings

Cook 4 ounces (115 grams) noodles in salted boiling water. Drain and add 2 tablespoons butter and 2 teaspoons toasted sesame seeds. Stir gently. Serve hot.

3. Stir in flour, salt, soy sauce, pepper and mushrooms. Cook for another 5 minutes.

4. Add undiluted soup. Simmer uncovered 10 minutes.

5. Stir in sour cream and minced parsley. Heat through.

CHICKEN WITH LEMON SAUCE

Fresh lemon flavor makes this dish outstandingly tasty.

INGREDIENTS: 4 servings

3 pounds (1¹/₃ kg) broiler-fryer chicken, cut-up
8 cups water
1-inch (2.5 cm) square ginger root
1 scallion, cut into 2-inch (5 cm)
{ 1 tablespoon cornstarch dissolved in 2 tablespoons water

Lemon Sauce:

Ⓐ {
¹/₂ cup water
¹/₂ teaspoon grated lemon peel
¹/₄ cup lemon juice
¹/₄ cup honey
1 tablespoon ketchup
¹/₂ teaspoon light-color soy sauce
1 clove garlic, finely chopped

Garnish:
1 lemon, sliced in thin rounds

1. Debone and cut chicken into serving pieces. Place the chicken pieces, ginger root, scallion and water in a pot. Bring to a full boil on high heat.

2. Skim and discard froth and fat, lower temperature to simmer, cover and simmer for one hour. Add water if necessary.

3. Bring Lemon Sauce ingredients Ⓐ to a boil. Stir in cornstarch mixture until sauce thickens. Cook and stir about 30 seconds. Place lemon slices on a platter and place chicken pieces on top. Pour Lemon Sauce over the chicken.

41

CHICKEN STEW, THAI STYLE

The pungent flavor of chili pepper and fresh coriander gives this stew its vibrant flavor and character.

INGREDIENTS: 4 to 6 servings

1 tablespoon coarsely chopped coriander root
1 tablespoon chopped garlic
1 teaspoon freshly ground pepper
1 chili pepper (fresh or dried)
1 tablespoon vegetable oil

A
{
2 tablespoons brown sugar
1/4 cup soy sauce
2 tablespoons fish sauce*
2 tablespoons *sake**
4 cups water
}

2 1/4 to 3 pounds (1 to 1 1/3 kg) fryer-broiler cut-up chicken
1 small zucchini, cut into 3/4-inch (2 cm) pieces
1 pound potatoes, (450 grams), cut into 1/2-inch (1.5 cm) slices
2 medium carrots, sliced
2 onions, cut into wedges

*Available at Oriental stores.

1. Prepare vegetables.

2. In a mortar, pound the coriander root, garlic and ground pepper and chili pepper to make a paste.

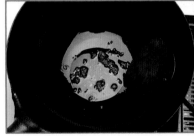

3. Heat 1 tablespoon oil in wok over medium heat and stir-fry the paste a few seconds until the aroma is released.

4. Add ingredients Ⓐ and bring to a boil. Pour the soup into a heavy pot.

5. Cut chicken into serving pieces. Add chicken pieces and all vegetables into the pot.

6. Simmer for 45 minutes or until chicken and vegetables are tender. Serve with hot cooked rice.

HOW TO CUT A CHICKEN

Place chicken, breast side up, on cutting board. Use a sharp knife.

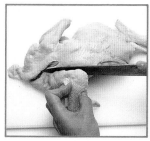

1. Cut off each leg by slicing skin between leg and breast; cut through the meat.

2. Pull one leg away from body until hip joint cracks. Remove leg from body by cutting through remaining skin. Repeat with the other leg.

3. Remove each wing by bending it back and cutting through joint, taking as much meat as possible from the back.

4. To separate back bone, place carcass on one side. Cut along each side of the backbone through the rib joint with poultry shears. Turn carcass and cut along other side to remove breast.

5. To separate drumstick from thigh, cut each drumstick from the fat line that runs crosswise at the joint between drumstick and thigh.

6. Repeat with the other side in the same manner.

7. Holding the chicken breast with both hands, bend it back to expose the breast bone. The bone should pop up. Run thumb down the breast bone and cartilage. Pull the entire bone and cartilage out. Trim off as much meat from the carcases as possible. Use the bones to make soup stock.

STEAMED GROUND CHICKEN BREAST WITH *TOFU*

A low-calorie, high-protein dish for calorie-conscious people.

INGREDIENTS: 4 servings

1 block (14 to 16 ounces, 400 to 450 grams) firm or soft *tofu*, well drained
¹/₂ pound (200 to 250 grams) ground chicken breast

Ⓐ
⎰ 1 tablespoon minced parsley
¹/₂ teaspoon salt
1 teaspoon *sake** or white wine
¹/₂ tablespoon lemon juice
Dash of pepper
⎱ 1 teaspoon light-color soy sauce

1 egg white

2 tablespoons cornstarch

Condiments: Lemon wedges
Ketchup
Hot mustard
Hot chili paste

*Available at Oriental stores.

Note: *Oil palm of your hand, shape mixture into balls and steam.*

1. Drain *tofu* well. Crumble *tofu*.

2. Mix *tofu* with ingredients Ⓐ. Mix well.

3. Beat egg white and mix with cornstarch. Combine *tofu* and egg white mixture.

4. Place plastic wrap in a mold, 6 × 5¹/₄ × 1³/₄-inch (15 × 14 × 4.5 cm), pour the *tofu* and chicken mixture into mold. Place mixture in a hot steamer for 13 to 15 minutes over medium heat. Turn up-side down and unmold.

STEAMED CHICKEN WITH SESAME SEEDS

INGREDIENTS: 4 servings

3 to 4 stalks fresh green asparagus
Pinch of salt
2 large whole chicken breasts, skinned and deboned
1 tablespoon *sake*
1 egg white
2 tablespoons cornstarch
1/2 cup each black and white toasted sesame seeds

The black and white sesame seeds provide textural contrast to the chicken breast.

1. Break or cut ends off asparagus stalks. Steam or boil for 5 minutes or until tender. Cut each chicken breast in half at the center. Butterfly each half by slicing breast from the outer edge, part way through, to open like a book.

2. Place each breast between pieces of plastic wrap and pound to flatten.

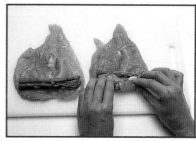

3. Place asparagus on the lower end of the breast. Roll up and secure with tooth picks.

4. Beat egg white lightly and mix with cornstarch; beat together.

5. Dip each roll into the mixture. Coat with sesame seeds.

6. Apply a thin film of oil over aluminum foil. Wrap each roll with the foil. Steam for 15 to 20 minutes over high heat. Remove tooth picks before slicing.

SZECHWAN STEAMED CHICKEN

Star anise and fresh ginger root bring out the distinctive flavor of the Szechwan region of China.

INGREDIENTS: 4 servings

3½ pounds (1.5 kg) broiler-fryer cut-up chicken or 2 large whole chicken breasts
1 teaspoon salt
3 anise stars*
1-inch (2.5 cm) square ginger root, sliced
1 clove garlic, sliced
Some *sake** or Hhao Hsing wine*
4-inch (10 cm) long leek or 1 bunch green onion, cut into 4-inch (10 cm) lengths

Condiments:
Oyster sauce
Lemon juice
Sesame sauce (1 tablespoon each sesame seeds, soy sauce and vegetable oil)

*Available at Oriental stores.

Note:
This dish can be served hot or cold

1. Soak anise stars in *sake* or wine. Rub 1 teaspoon salt into chicken skin. Place chicken on a large platter.

2. Top with anise stars, ginger, garlic and leek. Steam in a steamer for 20 to 25 minutes over high heat.

3. Allow to cool for a while. Slice for serving. Serve with sauce, soy sauce and hot mustard.

STEAMED *TOFU* LOAF

INGREDIENTS: 1 BOX

Makes 6 × 5¹/₄ × 1³/₄-inch (15 × 14 × 4.5 cm) loaf

2 blocks (16 ounces, each 450 grams) firm *tofu*, well drained

Ⓐ {
1 egg white, lightly beaten
1 teaspoon salt
1¹/₂ tablespoons cornstarch
}

5 ounces (140 grames) chicken breast, deboned and skinned

Ⓑ {
1 teaspoon *sake* or cooking wine
¹/₂ teaspoon soy sauce
Dash of pepper
¹/₈ teaspoon poultry seasoning
}

2 tablespoons minced green onion

This is a quick and easy hi-protein chicken dish.

1. Drain *tofu* well. Crumble *tofu* with fingers or electric mixer, add ingredients Ⓐ. Blend well until *tofu* is smooth in texture.

2. Thinly slice chicken breast. Marinate in ingredients Ⓑ.

3. Lay plastic wrap into loaf pan.

4. Pour half of *tofu* mixture. Sprinkle minced green onion on top. Place sliced chicken breast over green onion.

5. Place other half of *tofu* mixture and flatten out. Steam for 3 minutes over high heat. Turn heat to medium and continue steaming for 15 minutes. Add water if necessary during steaming. Slice into serving pieces.

STEAMED GROUND CHICKEN WITH MIXED VEGETABLES

A light, ginger-flavored ground meat adds the distinctive color with mixed vegetables.

INGREDIENTS: 1 Box

Makes 9 × 5 × 3-inch (23 × 13 × 8 cm) loaf
10 ounces (285 grams) finely ground chicken breast

Ⓐ
- 1½ teaspoons grated ginger root
- 1 teaspoon salt
- ½ tablespoon *sake*
- 4 teaspoons cornstarch
- 2 egg whites, slightly beaten
- 2 teaspoons soy sauce

1 hard boiled egg, sliced
½ cup cooked mixed vegetables
Some vegetable oil

1. Combine ingredients Ⓐ with ground chicken meat. Prepare a steamer.

2. Mix vegetables with meat.

3. Lightly grease a loaf pan; pour meat mixture in greased pan. Flatten the surface.

4. Place sliced egg as shown.

5. Steam for 15 minutes over high heat or until a bamboo skewer comes out clean after testing for doneness.

GROUND CHICKEN BREAST WITH ACORN SQUASH

Acorn squash, made attractive and colorful in combination with chicken.

INGREDIENTS: 4 servings

2 medium acorn squash
10 ounces (285 grams) finely ground chicken
  breast
Ingredients Ⓐ (see page 48)
1/2 cup cooked mixed vegetables

1. Cut squash lengthwise in two pieces leaving seeds in. Place on a paper towel and cook on HIGH(9) for 4 minutes.

2. Remove seeds and fibers.
3. Mix chicken meat with ingredients Ⓐ.
4. Spoon the chicken mixture into halved squash. Cook on HIGH(9) for 3 minutes. Turn position of the squash; cook on HIGH(9) for 4 more minutes. Cover it with paper towel; let stand for 5 minutes.
5. Season with butter, margarine or soy sauce.

CRISPY PETIT DRUMSTICKS

This recipe is ideal for a party served as a main dish or as an appetizer.

INGREDIENTS: Makes 16

16 drumsticks or 2 pounds (900 grams) chicken wings

Marinade Sauce:
1 teaspoon ginger juice
2 tablespoons soy sauce
$1/2$ tablespoon *sake*
1 green onion, minced

Cornstarch for coating
Oil for deep-frying

1. Separate wings at joints, discard tips. Remove the meat from the smaller end and push meat up, forming a small drumstick. The flat piece has two bones. Remove the smaller of the two bones. Push meat up from one end. Repeat this process with other wings.

2. Marinate the drumsticks for 30 minutes to one hour.

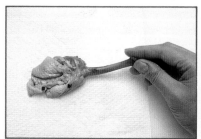

3. Wipe off excess sauce from drumsticks. Dust drumsticks with cornstarch. Deep-fry at 375°F (190°C) for 5 minutes or until golden brown.

DEEP-FRIED AND BARBECUED CHICKEN, THAI STYLE

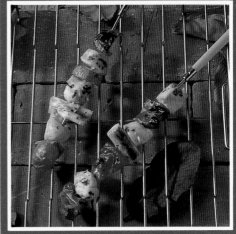

Some of the Thai dishes are extremely fiery. This fried chicken is soft and tender inside and the marinade sauce is sweetened with coconut milk.

Marinade Sauce*:

Makes ⅔ cup
3 tablespoons minced garlic
2 tablespoons fresh coriander (or ½ teaspoon ground coriander)
1 teaspoon turmeric
1 red pepper, seeded and coarsely chopped
1 teaspoon curry powder
1 tablespoon honey
Salt and pepper to taste
2 tablespoons fish sauce (imported)*
½ cup coconut milk
*Available at Oriental stores.

DEEP-FRYEDCHICKEN

4 servings
4 chicken legs
½ to ⅔ cup marinade sauce*
Flour for coating
Oil for deep-frying
1 tablespoon cornstarch plus 1 tablespoon water for thickening, 2 tablespoons each chopped green onion and fresh coriander leaves, ½ teaspoon sesame oil

BARBECUED CHICKEN

4 servings
3 pounds (1⅓ kg) chicken breast or drumsticks
½ to ⅔ cup marinade sauce*
2 green peppers, cut into 1-inch (2.5 cm) squares
2 zucchini, cut into 1-inch (2.5 cm) lengths
16 cherry tomatoes
1 onion, cut in to fourths and separate or leek, cut into 1-inch (2.5 cm) lengths.

1. Marinate the chicken legs in the sauce for several hours. Dust with flour. Deep-fry in 350°F (175°C) oil until golden.

2. In a small sauce pan, pour remaining sauce. Heat over medium heat, add cornstarch mixture to thicken the sauce and add sesame oil. Pour the sauce over the chicken. Sprinkle chopped green onion and coriander leaves.

1. Mix all marinade sauce ingredients. Cut chicken into small pieces. Marinate chicken in the sauce for several hours or overnight in the refrigerator. Divide chicken, green peppers, zucchini, tomatoes and onion into 8 equal portions.

2. Thread 8 skewers, alternating ingredients. Barbecue over hot coals for 10 minutes. Turn skewers over. Brush occasionally with the marinade sauce.

POTATO BALLS

A buffet supper is a good way to have a party. These proud potato balls taste as good as they look.

about 1-inch (2.5 cm) in diameter
4 mediuim potatoes
Salt and pepper to taste
2 tablespoons cornstarch
$^{1}/_{2}$ medium onion, finely minced
1 tablespoon oil
5 to 6 ounces (140 to 170 grams)
   ground chicken meat
$^{1}/_{4}$ each teaspoon salt and pepper
Some nutmeg
$^{1}/_{4}$ teaspoon poultry seasoning

Flour for dusting
1 slightly beaten egg
Bread crumbs for coating
Oil for deep-frying

Condiments:
   Mayonnaise
   Ketchup
   Worcestershire sauce
Optional Garnishes:
   Parsley
   Lemon wedges

1. In a sauce pan boil potatoes in salted water until fork-tender; drain. Remove skin. In a large bowl, mash potatoes; season with salt and pepper. Mix with cornstarch.

2. In a skillet, heat oil and stir-fry minced onion until soft.

3. Add ground chicken and remmaining ingredients.

Teatime Break

4. Mix with mashued potatoes. Form balls (walnut size).

5. Coat balls with flour, beaten egg and then bread crumbs in that order. Deep-fry in 360°F (180°C) oil until golden brown. Drain on wire rack.

INGREDIENTS: Bread Basket

1 large round French bread or any round bread
1 teaspoon crushed garlic
1 tablespoon butter or margarine

1. Preheat oven to 350°F (175°C). Melt butter or margarine over low heat and mix with crushed garlic. Cut the top fourth off the bread.

2. Remove all but ½-inch (1.5 cm) layer from inside of bread. Save the removed bread to make bread crumbs. Brush the inside of the bread with garlic butter.

3. Bake in 350°F (175°C) oven for 10 minutes or until edges turn golden. Arrange deep-fried potato balls in bread basket.

MASHED POTATOES

INGREDIENTS: 4 servings

3 medium potatoes, about 1 pound (450 grams)
¼ cup hot milk
2 tablespoons butter
1 teaspoon salt
Dash of pepper

1. Boil potatoes until done. When a fork or a skewer pierces a potato easily, it is done. Mash potatoes.

2. Add hot milk, butter, salt and pepper. Beat potatoes at medium speed until mixture is smooth.

SPRING ROLLS WITH CHEESE

INGREDIENTS: Makes 10 rolls

7 ounces (200 grams) chicken breast, deboned and skinned
10 slices Gouda cheese
10 spring roll wrappers

Oil for deep-frying

Gouda cheese, from Holland, gives a distinctive Dutch flavor to the spring rolls.

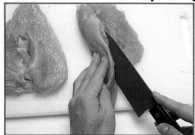

1. Slice chicken breast from the outer edge, part way through, to open like a book. Cut into 10 pieces.

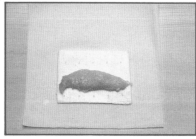

2. Place wrapper in front of you and put chicken and cheese slices on top.

3. Start to roll.

4. Fold sides in to overlap.

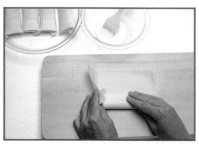

5. Fold sides in to overlap again.

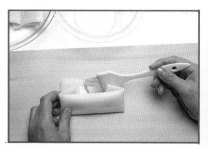

6. Place a small amount of flour and water mixture at top of wrapper to seal. Heat oil in wok to 350°F (170 to 180°C). Deep-fry rolls for 2 minutes or golden brown. Drain and let stand for a few minutes. Cut in half if you desire.

THAI SPRING ROLLS

20 spring roll wrappers
1 teaspoon freshly ground pepper
1 clove garlic, coarsely chopped
2 fresh coriander roots, coarsely chopped
2 tablespoons vegetable oil
5 ounces (140 grams) finely chopped chicken breast
1 Chinese sausage*, cut into julienne strips
1 ounce (30 grams) saifun noodles or bean-threads, soaked 5 minutes in warm water to soften, cut into 1 1/2-inch (4 cm) length
1/4 cup (100 grams) bamboo shoots, cut into julienne strips
1 tablespoon fish sauce*
1/2 tablespoon sugar
1/2 tablespoon cornstarch dissolved in 1 tablespoon water
2 tablespoons chopped fresh coriander leaves
Oil for deep-frying
*Available at Oriental stores.

Fresh coriander provides a delectable flavor.

1. In a mortar, grind garlic, pepper and coriander roots to make a paste.

2. Heat wok and add 2 tablespoons oil; add the paste to release the aroma. Add chicken, sausage, noodles and bamboo shoots. Stir-fry for 3 to 4 minutes.

3. Add fish sauce, sugar and cornstarch mixture to thicken.

4. Turn off heat; add chopped coriander leaves. Mix well.

5. Place about 1 heaping tablespoon of filling on the spring roll wrapper. Fold tip of wrapper over the meat.

6. Start to roll.

7. Fold sides in to overlap.

8. Roll wrapper and put a small dab of flour and water mixture to seal the ends. Deep-fry in 360°F (180°C) oil.

BREADED CHICKEN CUTLET

This delightful chicken cutlet is crisp on the outside and moist in the inside.

INGREDIENTS: 4 servings

2 large chicken breasts, deboned and skinned
$^2/_3$ cup all-purpose flour
2 eggs, slightly beaten
$1^1/_2$ cups bread crumbs
1 teaspoon paprika
1 teaspoon salt
Dash of pepper

Oil for deep-frying

Sauce:
$^1/_3$ cup Worcestershire sauce
2 tablespoons soy sauce
1 tablespoon ketchup
     Mix all ingredients.

Condiment: Hot mustard

1. Cut each chicken breast in half at the center. Pound it to flatten out.

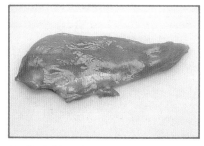

2. Sprinkle salt and pepper.

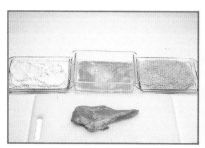

3. Dust with flour, roll in beaten eggs. Mix bread crumbs and paprika and press chicken breast in the bread crumbs. Deep-fry in 340°F (170°C) oil for 8 minutes or until golden brown. Serve with the sauce.

CHICKEN BREAST *TEMPURA*

The dipping sauce makes this dish extra special.

12 to 16 ounces (340 to 450 grams) chicken breast, deboned and skinned
2 green peppers
2 red peppers
Pinch of salt
1 teaspoon *sake*
3 egg whites
3 tablespoons cornstarch
Oil for deep-frying

Tempura Dipping Sauce:
Makes 1¹/₂ cups

1¹/₂ cups chicken stock
1 cup water or chicken stock
¹/₄ cup *mirin**
¹/₄ cup soy sauce

4 tablespoons grated *Daikon* radish

Garnishes: Lemon wedges
Grated *Daikon* radish
Condiments: Ketchup
Salt and pepper
Soy sauce

*Available at Oriental stores.

1. Cut chicken breast into small serving pieces. Sprinkle salt and 1 teaspoon *sake*. Set aside. Cut peppers into small chunks.

2. Beat egg whites with wire whisk; add cornstarch and beat to mix.

3. Heat deep-frying oil to 330°F (165°C). Dip chicken pieces into the beaten egg whites. Deep-fry until lightly browned, not golden brown. Repeat same process for peppers. Place grated *daikon* radish in a deep individual serving bowl. Arrange deep-fried chicken and peppers in bowl and pour hot sauce over.

ROAST CHICKEN

Roast chicken is an all-time international favorite.

INGREDIENTS: Makes 4 cups

Bread Stuffing
1 tablespoon butter or margarine
1 tablespoon vegetable oil
$\frac{1}{4}$ cup minced onion
4 cups coarse bread crumbs or day-old bread cubes
$\frac{1}{2}$ cup chopped celery (stalks and leaves)
1 teaspoon salt
$\frac{1}{4}$ teaspoon pepper
1 teaspoon dried thyme or marjoram
Some poultry seasoning
$\frac{1}{2}$ cup hot water

1. Heat butter or margarine and oil in skillet over medium heat. Add onion and cook until soft.

2. Stir in 1 cup bread crumbs. Cook over medium heat for 2 minutes.

3. Transfer into a deep bowl. Add remaining ingredients and mix.

4. Add ½ cup hot water to moisten crumbs.

Roast Chicken
3½ to 4 pounds (1.5 to 1.75 kg) roasting chicken
Some basil and pepper
Some vegetable oil

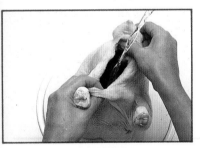

1. Wash and dry chicken.

2. Rub inside and outside of chicken with basil and pepper. Grease the chicken with a little vegetable oil. Stuff chicken lightly with bread stuffing. Stuffing should not be packed in.

3. Place chicken breast up, in shallow roasting pan.

4. Tie legs and tail. Do not add water. Do not cover. Place in oven. Roast in 375°F (190°C) oven, approximately 1½ to 2¼ hours.

Pan Gravy:
Add ½ cup water to pan and cook the gravy over moderate heat for a few minutes, stirring in all the brown bits. Season with salt and pepper.

Note:
When chicken turns golden, cover loosely with a 'tent' of folded foil.
Rice Stuffing: Follow the recipe above by replacing bread crumbs with cooked rice and add ½ cup water.

ROAST CHICKEN WITH YOGURT SAUCE

Chicken will never taste the same once you try this roast chicken prepared with yogurt and turmeric sauce.

INGREDIENTS: 4 servings

3 to 4 pounds (1⅓ to 1¾ kg) broiler-fryer chicken
2 teaspoons pepper
1 teaspoon ground ginger
Basting Sauce:
1 cup plain yogurt
1 cup heavy cream
2 onions, finely chopped
½ teaspoon poultry seasoning
½ tablespoon turmeric
¼ teaspoon salt

1. Wash and pat dry chicken. Prick the skin with a fork or a skewer.

2. Rub it with a mixture of pepper and ground ginger.

3. With string, tie legs and tail of chicken.

4. Place chicken breast side-up on rack in open roasting pan. Roast at 350°F (175°C) for 10 minutes. In a 2-quart sauce pan, heat basting sauce over medium heat.

5. Brush skin with sauce. Roast the chicken for about 1¹/₂ hours, basting frequently with sauce. Keep the sauce warm while basting.

Place the chicken on a heated platter, arrange rice or bread stuffing around it if you desire.

Mix some dripping from the roasting pan with yogurt sauce and pour some over the chicken.

Serve the remaining sauce separately.

CARVING ROASTED CHICKEN

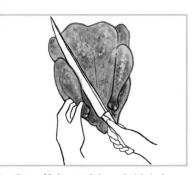

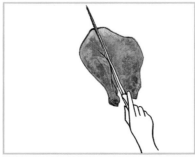

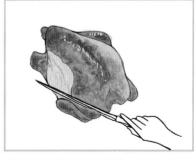

1. Cut off drumstick and thigh from body with sharp carving knife and slice through skin between leg and breast, making a quick slicing motion; sever at thigh joint.

2. Locate joint between drumstick and thigh; hold leg and bend to crack joint. Sever drumstick; thinly slice dark meat. Repeat with the other leg.

3. Insert fork securely into upper part of wing; make a horizontal incision at base of breast near neck to the bone after severing wing from breast.

4. Slice breast meat vertically. Follow bone contour to free meat near bone. Carve enough thin slices for serving.

5. Carve more as needed.

CHICKEN PIE WITH CREAMY SAUCE

Creamy sauce tops this pie dish.

INGREDIENTS: 4 to 6 servings

3 to 3¹/₂ pounds (1¹/₃ to 1¹/₂ kg) broiler-fryer cut-up chicken

Ⓐ {
4 cups water, pinch of salt, ¹/₂ teaspoon pepper corns
1 bay leaf
¹/₂ clove garlic
}

1 medium onion, cut into fourths
2 tablespoons minced celery
1 cup sliced carrot
2 tablespoons minced scallion
8 ounces (225 grams) sliced canned mushrooms, drained

Ⓑ {
4 tablespoons all-purpose flour
1²/₃ cups half-and-half cream
1 tablespoon *sake*
¹/₄ teaspoon dry mustard
¹/₂ teaspoon salt
}

2 sheets pastry for 9-inch (23cm) pie
Vegetable oil for coating baking dish
1 egg yolk

1. Preheat oven to 350°F (175°C).
In a 3-quart pot, place the chicken, water, salt, pepper corns, bay leaf and garlic and bring to a full boil on high heat. Turn heat to low and cook for 20 minutes, covered. Remove chicken. Allow to cool.
62

2. Strain soup stock with a fine mesh strainer or cheese cloth. Remove bones, skin and cartilage from chicken meat; cut into 1-inch (2.5 cm) pieces. Cook onion, celery and carrot in 1 cup soup stock over medium heat for 15 minutes, or until most of liquid is absorbed.

3. Mix chicken and cooked vegetables together.

4. In a large sauce pan, combine ingredients Ⓑ; pour 1¼ cups chicken stock carefully. Cook over low heat until sauce becomes creamy.

5. Add mushrooms, scallion, chicken and vegetables. Stir well.

6. Pour the filling in pastry-lined baking dish which has been lightly coated with vegetable oil.

Note:

Or press over rim with fork.
Cut 2 to 3 slashes in pie top to allow steam to escape. Lightly brush top of pie with egg yolk. Arrange some flower patterns on pie top and brush egg yolk on top. Bake in 350°F (175°C) oven for 1 hour.

7. Place one index finger on the inside edge of pastry and with index finger and thumb of other hand, pinch pastry to make flute.

8. Place pastry on top and trim edge.

CUT STYLE

SAVOY RICE PIE WITH GROUND CHICKEN SHELL

A delightful rice filling makes this dish a real conversation piece.

INGREDIENTS: 4 to 6 servings

1 pound (400 to 450 grams) ground chicken meat

Ⓐ {
  ½ cup bread crumbs
  ¼ cup chopped onion
  1 green pepper, chopped
  1 teaspoon salt
  ⅛ teaspoon oregano
}

2 cans (8 ounces, 225 grams each) tomato sauce

1 cup cooked chilled short or long grain rice

⅔ cup shredded cheddar cheese

½ teaspoon salt

Dash of pepper

1. Combine ground chicken meat with ingredients Ⓐ and one can of tomato sauce.

3. Combine rice, ¼ cup cheese, remaining tomato sauce, salt and pepper.

2. Spray cooking oil on pie plate; place chicken mixture. Pat mixture firmly over bottom and sides of 9-inch (23 cm) pie plate. Pinch 1-inch (2.5 cm) flutings around edge; set aside.

4. Spoon into meat shell; flatten on top. Cover with aluminum foil. Bake at 350°F (175°C) for 25 minutes. Remove foil cover, sprinkle remaining cheese over top; bake 10 to 15 minutes longer.

BAKED DRUMSTICKS WITH PARMESAN CHEESE

Crispy baked chicken is best when served piping hot.

INGREDIENTS: 4 servings

4 chicken drumsticks

Ⓐ
- 1¼ cups bread crumbs
- ¼ cup grated Parmesan cheese
- 1 teaspoon Italian seasoning
- ⅛ teaspoon paprika
- Salt and pepper to taste

Ⓑ
- 1 egg, slightly beaten
- 1 tablespoon water or milk

1. Preheat oven to 400°F (205°C). Wash and pat dry drumsticks. Combine ingredients Ⓐ in a paper or plastic bag.

2. Dip drumsticks in mixture Ⓑ.

3. Put one drumstick one at a time in the bag; shake to coat the chicken. Place the drumsticks on lightly greased baking sheet. Bake in oven for 40 to 50 minutes. Turn once or twice during baking.

PARTY PIZZA BREAD

Crusty French bread makes a fine miniature pizza.

INGREDIENTS: 4 to 6 servings

2 loaves French breads (about 10-inch, 25 cm) or 1 loaf
French bread (about 16-inch, 40 cm long)
4 tablespoons olive oil
1 cup spaghetti meat sauce
8 ounces (225 grams) cooked chicken meat, deboned,
skinned and chopped
$2/3$ cup chopped salami sausage
$1/3$ cup pimiento-stuffed green olives
1 cup grated Parmesan cheese
$1^1/2$ cups shredded Mozzarella cheese
1 green pepper, cut into rings

1. Cut bread lengthwise in half.

2. Remove center of breads save breads crumbs for other purpose.

3. Brush inside of the loaves with olive oil. Broil in oven until lightly browned. Set aside. Combine meat sauce, chicken meat and salami; place on the loaves.

4. Top with olives, Parmesan and Mozzarella cheese. Place under broiler and broil until cheese is melted, or bake in 350°F (175°C) oven for 20 minutes until cheese melts. Sauté the green pepper rings in the olive oil ; place on top of bread.
9 slice into equal pieces to serve.

66

CHICKEN *TERIYAKI*

One of the best known of all Japanese dishes is everyone's all time favorite.

2¹/₂ to 3 pounds (1¹/₃ to 1 kg) broiler-fryer cut-up chicken

***Teriyaki* Marinade Sauce :**
4 tablespoons soy sauce
1 teaspoon ginger juice or 1-inch (2.5 cm) square ginger root, grated
1 tablespoon *sake*
1 clove garlic, crushed
1 teaspoon sugar
1 tablespoon honey

1. Cut chicken into serving pieces. Mix ingredients sauce.

2. Marinate in the sauce for 1 hour. Cook chicken pieces in 375°F (190°C) oven for 45 minutes to 1 hour or until tender. Baste a few times with remaining marinade sauce.

CHICKEN QUICHE

Combination of cream of mushroom soup and cheese give this quiche its unique flavor and character.

INGREDIENTS: Makes 1 pie

9-inch (23 cm) in diameter

9-inch (23 cm) pastry shell
4 eggs
1/2 cup light cream
1 can (10 3/4 ounces, 305 grams) cream of mushroom
  soup, undiluted
1/2 cup diced cooked chicken meat
1/2 cup sliced mushrooms
1/2 cup cooked broccoli flowerets
1 cup shredded Cheddar or Mozzarella cheese
Ground nutmeg

1. Line the pastry shell into pie plate; set aside.

2. In a glass bowl, beat eggs until fluffy; combine light cream and mushroom soup. Combine chicken meat, sliced mushrooms, broccoli and cheese. Place on the pastry shell.

3. Pour cream mixture over the meat. Bake in preheated 350°F (175°C) oven for 50 minutes or until center is firm. Let sit for 10 minutes. Sprinkle ground nutmeg on top.

BAKED POTATO AND CHICKEN WITH CHEESE

Try this potato specialty with crusty French bread for a midday meal.

INGREDIENTS: 4 servings

$^1/_2$ pound (225 grams) cooked chicken meat, deboned and skinned
1 pound (450 grams) potatoes
1 stalk celery, chopped
1 medium size tomato, chopped
$1^1/_2$ cups frozen mixed vegetables
4 to 5 ounces (115 to 140 grams) Gouda cheese, grated
$^1/_2$ cup mayonnaise
Vegetable oil or butter
Paprika

1. Preheat oven to 350°F (175°C). Cut chicken meat into small pieces. Boil potatoes in salted boiling water until tender, about 30 minutes. Peel skin; cut into $^1/_2$-inch (1.5 cm) cubes. Cook frozen vegetables according to the package directions.

2. Mix chicken, potatoes, celery, tomato, and cooked vegetables. Mix 2 tablespoons grated cheese with mayonnaise. Toss into chicken mixture. Divide into fourths.

3. Grease a baking dish with oil or butter;place the mixture into dish. Sprinkle grated cheese on top. Bake in 350°F (175°C) oven for 5 to 6 minutes or until cheese melts.

69

GROUND CHICKEN TARTLETS

These miniature pastry shells filled with creamy cottage cheese and chicken can be served as tempting hot appetizers for a dinner party.

INGREDIENTS: Makes 12 tartlets

Instant pie crust mix or Pastry for 9-inch (23 cm) pie crust*

1 1/2 pounds (685 grams) ground chicken meat

Ⓐ {
1/2 cup chopped onion
1/2 teaspoon salt
1/2 teaspoon poultry seasoning
1/4 teaspoon pepper
1 clove garlic, minced
}

Ⓑ {
1 egg, slightly beaten
1 egg white, slightly beaten
2 cups cream-style cottage cheese
1/2 cup (2 ounces, 60 grams) grated processed Swiss cheese
}

* 1 cup all-purpose flour
1/2 teaspoon salt
1/4 cup plus 2 tablespoons shortening
3 tablespoons water

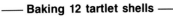
—— Baking 12 tartlet shells ——

1. Combine flour and salt in a mixing bowl. With pastry blender cut in shortening until little balls are formed.

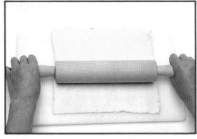

2. Sprinkle water and mix lightly until all flour is moistened. Form into a ball. Preheat oven to 400°F (205°C). Turn out onto surface which has been sprinkled with flour. Roll pastry to 1/2-inch (1.5 cm) thickness.

3. Cut dough into 12 pieces using a 3-inch (8 cm) round cutter.

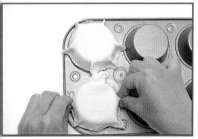

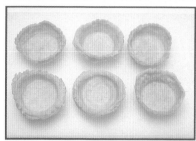

4. Grease the backs of round 12-cup muffin pan. Mold the round onto the back of pan, pressing lightly to seal. Prick top and side of crust to prevent puffing during baking.

5. Bake for 10 minutes. Set aside to cool.

6. Remove pastry shells from muffin pan. Place upright on cookie sheet.

— FILLING —

1. In a teflon-coated skillet, combine ground chicken and ingredients Ⓐ. Stir-fry until chicken and onion are cooked.

2. Drain off excess liquid.

3. Spoon ½ tablespoon chicken meat mixture into bottom of pastry shell.

4. Combine egg, egg white and cottage cheese. Spoon over meat mixture. Bake in over at 375°F (190°C) for 15 minutes. Top with Swiss cheese. Bake 10 minutes or until cheese melts.

VARIATION

Makes a 9-inch (23 cm) Pie Pastry

1 egg yolk, slightly beaten
2 cup biscuit mix
2 tablespoons milk

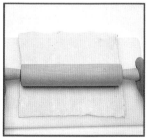

1. Stir together egg yolk, biscuit mix and milk. Form into a ball.

2. Turn onto surface sprinkled with flour. Roll out pastry to ½-inch (1.5 cm) thickness.

3. Carefully transfer pastry to a pie plate. Prick the pie shell all over with a fork so that air trapped below the shell escapes. Bake in oven at 400°F (205°C) for 10 minutes. Set aside to cool.

CHICKEN WITH ASPARAGUS

Fresh asparagus is baked in the oven with the parmesan cheese.

INGREDIENTS: Makes 1 pie	9-inch (23 cm) in diameter

8 large stalks asparagus
1 pound (450 grams) chicken breast, deboned and skinned
1 teaspoon lemon juice
1½ teaspoons soy sauce
8 pimiento-stuffed olives
1 tablespoon margarine, softened
⅔ cup bread crumbs
3 tablespoons white wine
3 tablespoons Parmesan cheese
1 tablespoon minced parsley

1. Snap or cut off the tough ends of the asparagus. Cook in salted boiling water until tender. After cooking asparagus dip in ice water to retain green color.

2. Cut the stalks into 1½-inch (4 cm) pieces.

3. Place chicken breast in a heat-proof dish. Sprinkle lemon juice and soy sauce. Steam the chicken for 10 minutes.

4. Slice the chicken breast into thinly 1½-inch (4 cm) long strips.

5. Mix bread crumbs with softened margarine. Slice olives.

6. Grease a baking dish.

7. Place chicken pieces in lightly greased baking dish or pie plate.

8. Place asparagus and olives over chicken.

9. Top with bread crumbs and Parmesan cheese. Sprinkle 3 tablespoons wine. Bake in 375°F (190°C) oven for 12 minutes or until lightly browned on top. Sprinkle with minced parsley.

CHICKEN ROLLS IN MUSHROOM SAUCE

INGREDIENTS: 4 servings

2 large whole chicken breasts
4 slices Swiss cheese
4 spinach leaves
$1/4$ each teaspoon salt and pepper
$1/4$ cup all-purpose flour
3 tablespoons vegetable oil

1 can ($10^3/4$ ounces, 305 grams) condensed cream of mushroom soup
$1/2$ cup water

This colorful dish is ideal for casual entertaining.

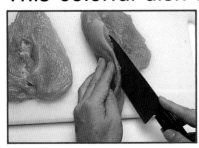

1. Cut chicken breast in half.

2. Place between 2 pieces of plastic wrap; pound with meat pounder to $1/4$-inch (7 mm) thickness, being careful do not tear meat.

3. Place a slice of cheese and spinach leaf onto chicken breast. Roll up and secure with a tooth pick.

4. Combine salt and pepper and flour; coat rolled chicken with flour.

5. In skillet heat 3 tablespoons oil over medium heat; add rolled chicken. Cook until all sides are lightly browned.

6. Place chicken into a microwave safe dish; pour condensed cream of mushroom soup and $1/2$ cup of water. Cover with plastic wrap; cook on full power HIGH(9) for 5 to 6 minutes. Allow to cool 5 minutes before serving. Remove tooth-picks.

HAWAIIAN CHICKEN

Coconut and banana slices add character to this dish.
This dish will be the delight of a party.

INGREDIENTS: 4 to 6 servings

12 × 7¹/₂-inch (30 × 19.5 cm) glass baking dish or casserole dish
2¹/₂ to 3 pounds (1¹/₄ to 1¹/₃ kg) broiler-fryer cut-up chicken, cut into
   serving pieces

Ⓐ
- 1 can (6 ounces, 170 grams) crushed or chunk pineapple
- 1 tablespoon cornstarch dissolved in 1 tablespoon water
- 1 tablespoon lime juice
- 1 tablespoon soy sauce
- 1 tablespoon sugar (optional)
- ¹/₄ teaspoon cinnamon

3 bananas, peeled and sliced
¹/₂ cup chopped macadamia nuts
¹/₂ cup coconut flakes, toasted

Note:

To toast coconut flakes, spread in glass pie plate. Cook in microwave oven on HIGH(9) for 5 to 6 minutes or until golden or toast in a teflon-coated skillet.

1. Place chicken pieces in glass dish, skin side down. Cover with wax paper, cook on HIGH(9) for 8 minutes. Turn the pieces over. Cook another 5 minutes.

2. Mix ingredients Ⓐ. Pour over chicken. Cover with wax paper.

3. Continue to cook on HIGH(9) for 10 minutes or until chicken is tender. Let set, 5 minutes. Arrange banana slices and nuts on top. Sprinkle toasted coconut flakes.

CHICKEN WINGS WITH HOISIN SAUCE

The pungent flavor of Hoisin sauce makes this dish special.

INGREDIENTS: 4 servings

24 ounces (685 grams) chicken wings or drumsticks
1 clove garlic, sliced

1 bunch green onions
2½ tablespoons Hoisin Sauce*
1 tablespoon rice vinegar*
2 tablespoons water
2½ teaspoons sugar
½ teaspoon grated ginger root, cut into 2-inch (5 cm)
   long pieces
½ teaspoon cornstarch
¼ teaspoon dry Chinese hot mustard*

2 tablespoons vegetable oil   *Available at Oriental stores.

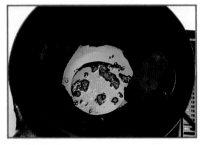

1. Chicken pieces. Heat 2 tablespoons oil in wok over medium heat; stir-fry garlic for 30 seconds.

2. Add chicken wings. Stir-fry for 7 minutes over medium heat; add green onion and stir-fry 2 to 3 minutes.

3. Add remaining ingredients and mix well. Heat until hot.

OYSTER SAUCE CHICKEN

This chicken dish goes especially well with hot steamed rice.

INGREDIENTS: 4 servings

24 ounces (685 grams) chicken, cut-up into serving pieces
1/2 tablespoon minced garlic
1 tablespoon sliced ginger root
12 ounces (340 grams) firm *tofu*, well drained
4 ounces (115 grams) whole canned mushrooms, drained
1/2 cup green peas, cooked
1 green onion, chopped
1 tablespoon oyster sauce*

1 tablespoon dry white wine or *sake**
1 teaspoon soy sauce
1/4 cup chicken broth
1 tablespoon cornstarch, dissolved in 1/4 cup water
2 tablespoons vegetable oil

*Available at Oriental stores.

1. Cut *tofu* into 1-inch (2.5 cm) cubes.

2. Heat 2 tablespoons oil in a wok over medium heat; stir-fry garlic and ginger root until aroma is released; add chicken. Stir-fry until golden brown, approximately 5 minutes.

3. Add *tofu*, mushrooms, oyster sauce, wine, soy sauce and chicken broth; heat until hot.

4. Add peas; pour corn-starch mixture. Stir and cook until thickened.

STIR-FRIED CHICKEN AND SNOW PEAS

Chicken wings make an elegant, low-cost and low-calorie main dish for an informal party.

INGREDIENTS: 4 servings

1½ pounds (685 grams) chicken wings

Ⓐ {
1 tablespoon *sake*
2 tablespoons soy sauce
1 teaspoon ginger root, grated
}

2 tablespoons cornstarch

2 scallion
6 ounces (170 grams) snow peas
2 tablespoons unsalted roasted nuts (peanuts or cashew)
1 clove garlic, sliced
5 tablespoons vegetable oil

Ⓑ {
2 tablespoons soy sauce
½ teaspoon sugar
1 tablespoon *sake*
¼ teaspoon Hot Chinese chili paste*
}

*Available at Oriental stores

1. Marinate wings in ingredients Ⓐ; set aside.

2. Cut scallion into 2-inch (5 cm) long pieces. String snow peas.

3. Heat 2 tablespoons oil in wok and stir-fry snow peas 2 to 3 minutes. Set aside.

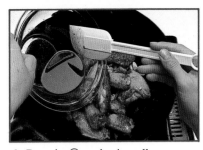

4. Add 3 tablespoons oil to wok; stir-fry sliced garlic over medium heat until aroma is released. Coat wings lightly with cornstarch and stir-fry until golden brown, 6 to 7 minutes.

5. Add scallion and nuts; stir-fry 2 to 3 minutes longer.

6. Pour in Ⓑ and mix well.

7. Add snow peas; turn off heat.

SOY SAUCE

Soy sauce is made from soy beans, and salt. Soy sauce gives a delicate flavor to foods. Japanese soy sauce contains 6.9% protein and 18% salt, and has approximately 10 calories per tablespoon. Chinese soy sauce is much stronger than Japanese soy sauce, so use Japanese soy sauce unless Chinese soy sauce is specifically indicated in any recipe. Check the labels when purchasing. Soy sauce has a shelf life of several years, though avoid exposure to light or heat.

REGULAR SOY SAUCE (Left):
This is the standard soy sauce. Color is dark.

LIGHT SOY SAUCE (Center):
The light soy sauce does not darken the colors of food and it is salty enough. It contains more salt than regular soy sauce.

LOW SODIUM SOY SAUCE (Right):
This soy sauce has less salt, yet has a delicate soy sauce flavor.

CHICKEN LIVERS WITH *TOFU*

Five spice powder is the key ingredient for this dish.

INGREDIENTS: 4 servings

½ pound (225 grams) chicken livers

Marinade Sauce:
1 teaspoon soy sauce
1 teaspoon ginger juice
1 teaspoon *sake*

2 tablespoons cornstarch for coating

12 ounces (340 grams) firm, *tofu*, well drained
2 tablespoons vegetable oil
½ clove garlic, minced
1 teaspoon chopped ginger root
1 medium onion

Cooking Sauce:
1 tablespoon soy sauce
¼ teaspoon sesame oil
⅛ teaspoon five spice powder*
1 teaspoon sugar
½ teaspoon salt

*Available at Oriental stores.

1. Wash and clean liver, changing water several times; cut into bite size pieces. Cut *tofu* into 1-inch (2.5 cm) cubes.

2. Marinate in marinade sauce for 30 minutes. Coat livers with cornstarch.

3. Heat 1 tablespoon oil in a wok; stir-fry garlic and ginger root over medium heat. Add livers and stir-fry and cook until brown on both sides. Remove from wok. Add 1 tablespoon oil in wok and heat until hot. Sauté onion until transparent; add *tofu* and stir-fry gently. Add livers and cooking sauce; bring to a boil.

BRAISED CHICKEN SZECHWAN STYLE

Hotness of Chinese chili paste may vary between different brands.

INGREDIENTS: 4 servings

8 small green peppers
1½ pounds (685 grams) chicken wings, thighs or legs
1 clove garlic, chopped

Ⓐ
  2 tablespoons *sake**
  2 teaspoons sugar
  2 heaping tablespoons red *miso*
  ½ to 1 teaspoon Chinese chili paste*
  2 tablespoons water
4 tablespoons vegetable oil

*Available at Oriental stores.

1. Cut around stem of green peppers; remove core, seeds and white membrane and dice it. Sprinkle 2 tablespoons *sake* on wings with wing tips chopped off.

2. Heat 2 tablespoons of oil in wok, and stir-fry garlic over medium heat. Add green peppers and stir-fry until soft for 2 to 3 minutes. Remove from wok and set aside.

3. Add 2 tablespoons oil to wok; stir-fry wings over medium heat. Combine ingredients Ⓐ; pour over chicken. Cook until chicken is tender; add green peppers and mix well. Turn the wings during cooking to prevent the sauce from burning.

GRUEL RICE

Rice is a staple food of the Orient. Today this method of cooking rice in a lot of water is very popular among Japanese and Chinese.

INGREDIENTS: 4 servings

Two chicken thighs
$9^1/_2$ cups water
1 teaspoon *sake*
$^1/_2$-inch (1.5 cm) square ginger root

$1^1/_4$ cups short grain rice
Salt to taste
1 teaspoon *sake*

Garnishes: Minced scallion
Seven spice powder
Condiments: Salt and pepper
Soy sauce

1. Rinse and drain chicken thighs. In a large pot place chicken, water, *sake* and ginger root. Cook on high and bring the chicken to a boil. Turn heat to medium and cook until tender, skimming froth during cooking.

2. Let it cool. Keep pot in a refrigerator overnight. The next day, remove grease from stock. Remove bones and skin from thighs; shred into serving pieces.

3. Rinse and drain rice. In a 3-quart pot, cook rice with 8 cups stock and 1 teaspoon *sake* over low heat for an hour. Add shredded chicken. Season with salt if you desire. Sprinkle minced scallion on top.

CHICKEN-RICE SALAD WRAPPED IN LEAF

This salad dish is inspired from the Korean "Milsam". "Sam" refers to the wrapping ingredients.

INGREDIENTS: Makes 4 rolls

3 cups cooked rice (see page 100)
4 leaves of lettuce, such as Romaine, red leaf lettuce
4 ounces (115 grams) bamboo shoots
3 medium *shiitake* mushrooms

5 ounces (140 grams) chicken breast, skinned and deboned
Ⓐ { 1 teaspoon *sake*
1/2 teaspoons soy sauce
Ginger juice to taste

Ⓑ { 3 tablespoons vegetable oil
1/2 tablespoon red or white *miso** (soy been paste)
1/2 tablespoon soy sauce
1/2 tablespoon *sake*
1 teaspoon sugar

*Available at Oriental stores.

Note:
This dish can be served hot or cold. Hot cooked rice can be seasoned with salt and toasted sesame seed mixture.

1. Slice chicken breast into julienne strips, 1/4-inch (7mm) long. Marinate in *sake*, soy sauce and ginger juice. Combine ingredients Ⓑ. Slice bamboo shoots and mushrooms into julienne strips.

2. Heat wok oven medium heat; pour 2 tablespoons oil. Stir-fry seasoned chicken breast until meat turns white in color. Add 1 tablespoon oil, bamboo shoots and *shiitake* mushrooms. Stir-fry for 2 to 3 minutes.

3. Pour in ingredients Ⓑ. Stir-fry for a few seconds. Place a leaf lettuce on serving plate; arrange rice and cooked chicken. Wrap lettuce leaf around fillings.

CHICKEN-AND-RICE CASSEROLE

This is a charming colorful rice dish, flavored with Japanese seasonings.

INGREDIENTS: 4 to 6 servings

2½ cups rice
½ pound (225 grams) chicken breast, deboned and skinned
1 tablespoon soy sauce
½ tablespoon *sake*
½ small carrot
3 ounces (85 grams) bamboo shoots
3 medium aried *shiitake* mushrooms, softened
4 water chestnuts (canned)

1 cup frozen peas, cooked
3¼ cups soup stock
1 teaspoon salt
1 teaspoon light-color soy sauce
1 teaspoon *mirin* (Japanese sweet cooking wine)

Note:
rice cooking instructions see page 100.

1. Wash rice; drain.

2. Slice chicken breast into julienne strips; marinate in soy sauce and *sake*. Set aside.

3. Cut carrot, bamboo shoots.

84

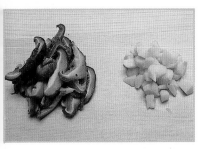

4. Cut mushrooms into julienne strips. Cut water chestnuts into fourths.

5. In a 3-quart pot or Dutch oven, cook chicken, carrot, bamboo shoots, *shiitake* mushrooms and water chestnuts over high heat until it comes to a boil. Add salt, soy sauce and *mirin*; bring to a boil.

6. Strain ingredients.

7. In a rice cooker or Dutch oven, pour in strained liquid and rice. Cook the rice, covered. Turn off heat. Toss in cooked ingredients. Let stand for 10 minutes.

8. Add cooked green peas. Fluff rice to serve.

VARIATION

CHICKEN *SUSHI*

Rice is seasoned with Japanese rice vinegar, sugar and salt.

3½ cups *sushi* rice (see page 100)
1½ ounces (44 grams) carrot
⅓ cup cooked peas
2 dried *shiitake* mushrooms

Ⓐ
⎧ ¼ cup *dashi* stock
⎪ ¼ cup *shiitake* soaking water
⎨ 2 tablespoons *mirin* (Japanese
⎪   sweet cooking wine)
⎪ 1½ tablespoons soy sauce
⎩ 1 tablespoon *sake*

1¾ ounces (50 grams) lotus root

Ⓑ
⎧ 2 tablespoons sugar
⎪ 3 tablespoons rice vinegar
⎨ ½ teaspoon salt
⎩ 1 teaspoon alum

7 ounces (200 grams) chicken
breast, skinned and deboned
1½ tablespoons *teriyaki* sauce (see
page 87)
4 large eggs

Ⓒ
⎧ ¼ cup milk
⎨ ⅔ teaspoon salt
⎩ Dash of pepper

1. Peel carrot and cut into 1-inch (2.5 cm) long matchsticks. Cook carrots in Ⓐ.

2. Soak *shiitake* mushrooms until soft. Trim off stems and slice thinly add to Ⓐ.

3. Peel lotus root, slice into ⅛-inch (5 mm) thick rounds. Soak in alum (or vinegar) and water solution. In a saucepan, mix Ⓑ. When boiling add lotus slices. Cook for 10 minutes over low heat.

4. Marinate chicken in *teriyaki* sauce for 1 hour.

5. Grill or broil chicken. Cut chicken into cubes.

6. To make scrambled eggs: break 4 eggs into a bowl, and add ©. Beat well.

7. Melt 1 tablespoon butter or magarine in 10-inch (25 cm) skillet and pour in scrambled eggs. Scramble with spatula.

8. Mix process number 1, 2, 3, 5 and 2 tablespoons peas, with *sushi* rice.

9. Put ¼ of rice mixture into heart-shaped mold. Decorate with peas and scrambled eggs.

HOW TO MAKE *TERIYAKI* SAUCE

Makes about ¼ cup

1. Pour soy sauce into a bowl.

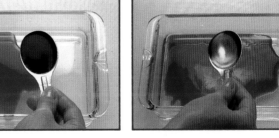

2. Add *mirin*.

For 1 pound (450 grams) of meat

4 tablespoons soy sauce
1 tablespoon *mirin*, Japanese sweet cooking wine
1 clove garlic, crushed
2 teaspoons ginger root, chopped
1 teaspoon salt

☆ *Teriyaki* sauce will keep for 1 week in refrigerator.

3. Add chopped ginger root.

4. Add crushed garlic (use garlic press).

CHICKEN PILAF WITH PAPRIKA

The combination of chicken and rice goes well with a touch of paprika.

INGREDIENTS: 4 servings

2¹/₂ cups short or long grain rice
2¹/₂ cups water
1¹/₂ teaspoons salt

2 large whole chicken breasts, deboned and skinned
2¹/₂ tablespoons minced onion
1 tablespoon raisins
2 tablespoons butter or margarine
1 tablespoon paprika
Salt and pepper to taste
5 ounces (140 grams) peas, cooked
6 pimiento-stuffed green olives

1. Wash, rinse and drain rice. Cut chicken breasts into small bite size pieces.

2. In a Dutch oven, melt butter or margarine and sauté onion until soft over medium heat. Add chicken; stir-fry until chicken turns white. Add rice; stir-fry for 1 to 2 minutes.

3. Pour 2¹/₂ cups water, salt and pepper, raisins and paprika. Cover and cook for 12 to 14 minutes. Reduce heat to low after boiling. Turn off heat; leave for 10 minutes, covered. Fluff rice and mix green peas and olives.

CHICKEN FRIED RICE

INGREDIENTS: 4 servings

3 cups cooked rice (see page 100)
3 dried *shiitake* mushrooms
1 green onion
8 ounces (225 grams) cooked chicken
  meat, diced
2 eggs, lightly beaten
Salt to taste
1$\frac{1}{2}$ tablespoons vegetable oil
2 tablespoons vegetable oil for stir-frying
$\frac{1}{3}$ cup mixed frozen vegetables, cooked
Salt to taste
Dash of pepper
$\frac{1}{2}$ teaspoon light-color soy sauce (optional)
$\frac{1}{4}$ teaspoon curry powder
2 tablespoons vegetable oil for stir-fry rice

One of the best-known Chinese dishes, this recipe makes a great hurry-up lunch.

1. Soak *shiitake* mushrooms in warm water to soften. Trim off hard stem ends. Mince coarsely. Chop green onion and cooked chicken into small pieces.

2. In wok heat 1$\frac{1}{2}$ tablespoons oil over medium heat.

3. Pour beaten eggs and scramble gently until eggs are set and fluffy. Set aside.

4. Pour 2 tablespoons oil in wok, stir-fry chicken pieces, *shiitake* mushrooms, green onion and mixed vegetables. Season with salt and pepper. Add curry powder and soy sauce. Set aside.

5. Pour in another 2 tablespoons oil in wok, stir-fry rice to heat through over medium heat for a minute.

6. Add scrambled eggs and chicken vegetable mix; stir-fry for 30 seconds over medium heat.

COLD NOODLES WITH VEGETABLES

INGREDIENTS: 4 servings

$^1/_2$ pound (225 grams) Chinese noodles
$^1/_2$ teaspoon sesame oil
7 ounces (200 grams) cooked chicken breast, deboned and skinned
2 to 3 sheets of egg omelet*
2 Japanese cucumbers
1 small carrot
8 ounces (225 grams) beansprouts
$^1/_2$ stalk celery

Sauce:

$1^1/_4$ cups chicken stock
$^1/_2$ cup sugar
$^1/_2$ cup soy sauce
$^1/_2$ cup rice vinegar
1 teaspoon sesame oil
1 teaspoon ginger juice
Chili oil (optional)

The flavor is enhanced with sesame oil and rice vinegar.

1. Boil noodles until tender. Rinse in cold water, drain. Place noodles in a bowl; sprinkle $^1/_2$ teaspoon sesame oil. Set aside or keep in a refrigerator.

2. Slice cooked chicken breast. Slice omelet into strips. Cut cucumbers, celery and carrot into 2-inch (5 cm) long julienne strips. Cook beansprouts in lightly salted water for 2 minutes; drain. Chill vegetables.

3 Mix all sauce ingredients together. Arrange chilled noodles on serving dish and top with chicken and vegetables. Serve with sauce.

Egg Omelet:
2 large eggs
1 teaspoon cornstarch
1 teaspoon water
Pinch of salt
Vegetable oil

1. Break eggs into a bowl. Mix cornstarch, water and salt together. Beat eggs and add cornstarch mixture. Mix well.

2. In teflon-coated skillet. Grease with a small amount of oil and heat over medium-low and pour in eggs to coat all bottom surface. Cook over medium heat. Slide out onto wax paper.

HOT NOODLES WITH SPINACH

A hearty noodle dish, traditionally served as lunch in Japan.

INGREDIENTS: 4 servings

¹/₄ pound (115 grams) thick noodles (*Udon*)*
7 ounces (200 grams) chicken wings or thighs, deboned and cut into bite size pieces
1 bunch fresh spinach
4 *shiitake* mushrooms*
¹/₂ leek
8 sliced fish cake*
1 hard boiled egg, sliced

Soup Stock:
5 cups chicken stock
1 tablespoon *sake*
1 tablespoon *mirin* (Japanese sweet cooking wine*)
¹/₄ cup light-color soy sauce
¹/₂ teaspoon sugar
Salt to taste

*Available at Oriental stores

1. Cook noodles in boiling water until soft. Rinse, drain and place in 4 individual serving bowls. Keep warm.

2. Cook spinach in salted boiling water; rinse, drain. Cut into 2-inch (5 cm) long pieces. Divide into fourths. Slice mushrooms thinly, parallel to the stem, and cut leek into diagonal slices, 2-inch (5 cm) long.

3. Bring soup stock to a boil, adding chicken pieces, mushrooms and leek until chicken pieces are tender for 10 minutes over medium heat. Pour over noodles and garnish with spinach, fish cake slices and egg slices.

STIR-FRIED NOODLES WITH RED PEPPER FLAKES

Crunchy peanuts and a touch of red pepper flakes are the secret ingredients.

INGREDIENTS: 4 servings

8 ounces (225 grams) soft chow mein noodles (steamed Chinese noodles) or dried noodles
3 to 4 tablespoons vegetable oil
2 tablespoons chopped garlic
1/4 pound (115 grams) ground or finely chopped boneless and skinless chicken breast
1 cup beansprouts
1/4 cup coarsely chopped peanuts
1/4 cup dried shrimp*
2 tablespoons sweet pickles, chopped
2 tablespoons fish sauce*
2 teaspoons sugar
1 teaspoon red pepper flakes
1/2 lime, squeezed
3 green onions, cut into 1-inch (2.5 cm) length

Condiments (optional):
Lime wedges
1 tablespoon each red and green chili peppers
*Available at Oriental stores.

1. Boil noodles in lightly salted water until soft; drain.

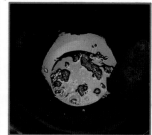

2. Heat oil in wok over medium heat. Add garlic; stir-fry for 1 minute.

3. Add the chicken and stir-fry for 3 to 4 minutes.

4. Add beansprouts.

5. Add noodles, stir well.

6. Add remaining ingredients, stir-fry 6 to 7 minutes, being careful not to break the noodles. Serve with condiments if you desire.

BARBECUE PARTY

Let's Enjoy the Barbecue Party!!

Basic Sauce

Combine all ingredients.

INGREDIENTS:

Makes ½ cup

3 tablespoons sugar
3 tablespoons *sake*
3 tablespoons *mirin*, Japanese sweet
  cooking wine*
3 tablespoons soy sauce
1 clove garlic, crushed
1-inch (2.5 cm) square ginger root,
  grated

*Available at Oriental stores.

Tomato-Sauce-Based Barbecue Sauce

INGREDIENTS: Makes 2 cups
2 tablespoons chopped onion
2 tablespoons chopped green
  pepper
1 tablespoon vegetable oil
1 can (8 ounces, 225 grams) tomato
  sauce
1 tablespoon soy sauce
1 tablespoon water
¼ cup rice vinegar
1 tablespoon Worcestershire sauce
2 tablespoons brown sugar
1 tablespoon paprika
1 teaspoon dry mustard
½ teaspoon salt
¼ teaspoon chili powder
⅛ teaspoon cayenne pepper
Process:
1. Sauté onion and green pepper in 1
tablespoon oil until onion is transparent.
2. Add remaining ingredients; heat
through. Allow to cool.

Mild Sauce

INGREDIENTS:

1. Combine all sauce ingredients.
Remove bones and cut each chicken
breast into halves at the center. Butterfly each half by slicing breast from the
outer edge, part way through, to open like
a book for a thick breast meat. This is
to hasten cooking. Pierce skin two to
three places.

2. Place half of the sauce in shallow
rectangular dish; place chicken breasts
side by side. Pour the remainder of
sauce over chicken. Cover with plastic
wrap and marinate for several hours in
refrigerator. Remove thew sauce from
meat. Broil or grill.

Note:
*This sauce can be used two to three more
times by adding* sake *and* miso.

Thick And Mild *Teriyaki* Sauce
INGREDIENTS: Makes about 1 cup
⅓ cup *mirin*, Japanese sweet cooking wine*
⅓ cup soy sauce
1½ to 2 tablespoons sugar
1 teaspoon honey
Process:
1. In a small sauce pan heat *mirin*, soy
sauce, sugar and honey over medium
heat until sugar dissolves and sauce becomes thick. Soaking skewers in water
prevents burning when grilling. Skewer
chicken and vegetables alternately.

*Available at Oriental stores.

Makes about ¼ cup

For 2 large whole chicken breast
14 ounces (400 grams) red *miso**
½ to 1 teaspoon Chinese chili
  paste*
¼ cup *sake* or cooking wine
1 teaspoon sugar

*Available at Oriental stores.

Lemon Flavored Sauce

INGREDIENTS:

Makes ½ to ⅔ cup

4 tablespoons olive oil
1-inch (2.5 cm) square ginger root, grated
1 colove garlic, crushed
½ teaspoon marjoram
¼ teaspoon dried thyme leaf
½ teaspoon grated lemon peel
¼ cup lemon juice
1 tablespoon Chinese coriander
1 teaspoon paprika
1 teaspoon soy sauce
¼ teaspoon salt
Dash of pepper

Hot and Spicy Sauce

INGREDIENTS:

Makes 2 cups

4 tablespoons each red and white *miso*
  (soy bean paste)
1 clove garlic, crushed
½ scallion, minced
2½ tablespoons sesame oil
½ tablespoon chili pepper
1 cup soy sauce
2 tablespoons Kochu Jang (hot Korean
  sauce)
1 teaspoon grated ginger juice
¼ medium apple, grated
¼ cup each *sake* and *mirin*, Japanese
  sweet cooking wine
2½ tablespoons water
3 ounces (85 grams) sugar

SKEWERS

1. Soaking shewers in water prevents burning.

2. Skewer ingredients alternately.

Marinade Sauce for Giblets

INGREDIENTS:

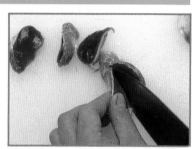

2. Brush glaze over skewered giblets several times while grilling.

½ pound (225 grams) giblets
1 tablespoon each of *sake* and *mirin*
2 tablespoons soy sauce
1 teaspoon grated ginger juice

1. Marinate giblets, in the sauce for 10 minutes; skewer pieces and grill.

Barbecue Hints

Preheat grill well, then put meat on. Turn when one side is done. Never recook again especially for thinly sliced meat as the meat loses its flavorful juice and becomes too crusty.

It is recommended that vegetables also be grilled for nutritive balance.

LUNCH BOX IDEAS

Chicken *Teriyaki* with French-Fried Potatoes
This is an attractive lunch for a family picnic.

Chicken *Teriyaki* (see page 67).

Spring Rolls with Jellied Chicken Salad
This makes a tasty filling lunch with soup.

Spring Rolls with Cheese (see page 54)
Thai Spring Rolls (see page 55)
Jellied Chicken Salad (see page 12)

Roast Chicken with Jellied Chicken Salad
Roasted chicken fits perfectly in an informal party menu.

Roasted Chicken (see page 58)
Jellied Chicken Salad (see page 12)
Edible Chrysanthemum, steamed and seasoned with salt and
pepper

Chicken Balls with Mashed Potatoes
These nutritious chicken balls will be one of all-time
favorites.

Chicken Balls (see page 52)
Mashed Potatoes (see page 53)

Information

MENU PLANNING

Basic Rules

1. Seasonal appropriateness
Special attention should be given to the ingredients you choose. Some fresh fish and vegetables are available only at certain times of the year. Therefore, consider using seasonal ingredients which are abundant in the market.

2. Occasion
To serve a Japanese meal does not have to be so tedious. There are many one-pot dishes cooked on the table.
Consider the number of people you serve and whether you serve for festive occasions, luncheon, dinner, picnic, etc.

3. Flavor and Texture
Plan your menu with meat, fish and vegetables. Make each dish with a different cooking method, such as grilled, steamed, fried, etc.

4. Color
Presentation of food is also important. Each ingredient has a different flavor, texture and color. It is important to appeal to the eyes as well as to the tongue.

5. Nutrition
It helps when determining the kind of food to serve to find out the diner's physical conditions and age.

6. Cost
Seasonal fresh items generally have lower prices. See the weekly specials for your menu planning.

Preparation

Step I
1. Read recipes carefully and thoroughly.
2. Write down all necessary ingredients you need to buy.
3. Check all cooking equipment and place within reach.
4. Arrange all necessary seasonings, spices and herbs on kitchen counter or within your reach.
5. Prepare measuring cups and spoons.
6. Prepare all serving bowls, plates and platters near you. You may need to keep some serving platters warm.

Step II
1. Put comfortable clothes on and wear an apron, so that you will be psychologically ready for cooking.
2. Prepare plenty of kitchen towels and paper towels.

Step III
Hot food should be placed on warmed plate and cold food on chilled plate. Also look at the design on the plate if any before you place food on it. Place the plate so that the design faces the diner. With towel, wipe off around the rim if there are spilled bits or traces of liquid.

PREPARATION

How To Select And Store Poultry

Poultry, whether purchased fresh or frozen, should be labeled with packer's brand name, weight, price and USDA INSPECTED PASSED SEAL. Store fresh poultry loosely wrapped in refrigerator; use within two days. Store frozen poultry in freezer; date the label and use within 6 months. Thaw frozen poultry completely before cooking; either unwrapped in refrigerator overnight or unwrapped in cold water one to two hours until meat is pliable. Allow about two hours per pound to thaw in the refrigerator. Wash chicken as soon as you get home, or soak it in cold water with a little salt. Rinse thoroughly and blot dry with paper towel. If you are not going to use it the same day, rub a cut lemon all over chicken (the acid in the lemon will keep it fresh smelling). Place chicken in a nonaluminum bowl, cover and refrigerate overnight.

Don't buy more food than you can use in a short time. Cheaper by the dozen isn't valid if the food spoils. For Roasting, plan to purchase $3/4$ pound (340 grams) per person ready-to-cook weight. For Pan-frying or Oven-baking, choose quatered or cut-up broiler-fryer. If your fryer weighs just $1^1/4$ pounds (565 grams), fry all of it. If it is nearer 3 pounds (1350 grams), save breast to cook separately. For Stewing, buy a chicken that is meaty, but not too fat. Stewing chickens are hard to find in some localities; if so, select a heavy roaster or broiler-fryer.

Turkey: Allow $1/2$ to $3/4$ pound (225 to 340 grams) ready-to-cook weight per serving plus a generous amount.

How To Cut A Chicken

Place chicken, breast side up, on cutting board. Use a sharp knife.

1. Cut off each leg by slicing skin between leg and breast. Cut through the meat. Pull one leg away from body until hip joint cracks. Remove leg from body by cutting through remaining skin. Repeat with other leg.
2. Cut each drumstick away from thigh, hold leg in both hands and bend to crack joint. Cut through the joint between drumstick and thigh.
3. Cut off each wing by bending it back and cutting through joint.
4. To separate back bone, place carcass on one side. Cut along each side of the backbone through the rib joints with poultry shears. Turn carcass and cut along other side to remove breast.
5. Place breast skin side down. Divide breast lengthwise in two, bending it back both sides to snap the breast bone. Pull out bone and cartilage.
6. Boning a chicken breast, with sharp knife, working with outer edge of breast, cut parallel to large end of rib bone and scrape meat away from bone and rib cage.
   Repeat with remaining side of breast.
7. Cut each whole chicken breast into halves at the center.
8. The skin is easily removed.
9. Remove layer of fat under the skin.

Rice Cooking

There are two types of rice available; white short-grain rice and white long-grain rice. Use white short-grain rice for Japanese dishes. The short-grain rice is more glutinous than the long-grain rice. In the U.S., short-grain rice is grown extensively in California. Newly cropped rice needs less water and slightly shorter cooking time than old rice. A little practice is needed to make perfect rice, however if you cook a lot of rice, an automatic rice cooker will make your work a lot easier, so it's a good investment.

Rice increases in volume as it cooks, twice to three times, depending on the kind of rice you use. The following is a key to shiny and fluffy rice. Go ahead with these basic tips for successful rice cooking. It's easy.

1. Measure rice carefully.
2. Wash rice in a big bowl of water. Rub grains gently since wet grains break easily.
3. Remove any bran or polishing agent. Drain off water well. Repeat this step until water is almost clear.
4. To make fluffy and moist rice, set rice aside for at least 30 minutes in summer and one hour in winter. This allows ample time for rice to absorb water.
5. In cooking pot, add rice and correct amount of water. Cover with lid.
6. Cook rice over medium heat until water boils. Do not bring it to boiling point quickly. If the quantity of rice is large, cook rice over high heat from the beginning. The heat can be carried into the center of rice if cooked over medium heat.
7. When it begins to boil, turn heat to high and cook for 1 minute. Never lift lid while cooking.
8. Turn heat to low and cook for 4 to 5 minutes (Be careful not to overboil). Then the pot begins to steam.
9. Reduce heat to the lowest for 10 minutes.
10. Turn off the heat and let rice stand covered for 10 minutes. During these 10 minutes the grains are allowed to "settle", and the cooking process is completed by the heat retained in the rice and the walls of the pot.

How To Make *Sushi* Rice

Prepare a non-metallic tub, preferably wooden or glass (make sure it is not polished since the vinegar will remove the wax polish).

1. Wash mixing tub well. Dry with kitchen towel.
2. Put cooked rice into mixing tub and spread evenly over the bottom of mixing tub.
3. Sprinkle vinegar mixture generously over the rice. You may not need all of vinegar mixture. Do not add too much liquid.
4. With a large wooden spoon, mix rice with a slicing motion.
5. While you mix, fan using the other hand or an electric fan. This is not to cool *sushi* rice, but to puff the extra liquid away.
6. Keep *sushi* rice in the wooden tub, covered with a damp cloth.

Cooked Rice

COOKED RICE	Rice	Water
2½ C	1 C	1¼ C
5 C	2 C	2½ C
7½ C	3 C	3¼ C
10 C	4 C	5 C

Sushi Rice

COOKED RICE	Rice	Water	PREPARED *SUSHI* RICE	VINEGAR MIXTURE		
				Vinegar	Sugar	Salt
2½ C	1 C	1⅕ C	2½ C	2 T	½ T	1 t
5 C	2 C	2 C	5 C	3½ T	1 T	1½ t
7½ C	3 C	3-3¼ C*	7½ C	5 T	1½ T	2 t
10 C	4 C	4-4½ C*	10 C	7 T	2 T	3t(1T)

C=cup   T=tablespoon   t=teaspoon
*makes softer rice.
The above vinegar mixture proportions are the basic recipe.
Sugar can be increased for a sweeter taste.

PREPARATION

Basic Cutting Methods

When preparing ingredients use a sharp knife. Cut to bite size pieces making them easy to cook, and eat. For decorative cuts, use the tip of knife. For peeling use the lower part of blade. The part from the center towards the tip is used for most cutting work.

Diagonal Slices	**Dices**	**Mincing**	**"Paring" Thin Fillets**	**Quarter Rounds**

Thin round ingredients such as cucumber are sliced diagonally giving a large surface.	Ingredients are cut into ³/₈-inch (1 cm) wide sticks, and then into ³/₈-inch (1 cm) cubes.	Ingredients such as ginger root or green onion are shredded and chopped finely.	Soft or fragile ingredients are placed flat and pared off with the knife parallel to the cutting board.	Large round ingredients such as turnip or *daikon* radish are split into quarters and then sliced.

Rolling Wedges	**Rounds**	**Shreds**	**Sticks**	**Wedges**
				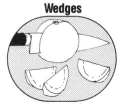
Ingredients are rolled and cut diagonally to give more sides for seasoning.	Round ingredients such as *daikon* radish or carrot are cut into the same thickness.	Ingredients are sliced into thin rectangles of 2–2¹/₂-inch (5–6.5 cm) length, layered and cut into thin matchlike sticks parallel to the fibers.	Ingredients such as potato, carrot or bamboo shoots are cut into 2–2¹/₂-inch (5–6.5 cm) long, ³/₈-inch (1 cm) wide sticks.	Ingredients such as lemon or onion are split into quarters or eighths.

TOFU PREPARATION TIPS

Fresh *tofu* is very fragile.

It is best to use fresh *tofu* within 24 hours after it is made. If it is not to be used right away, drain out water from the original container; add cold water and seal tight. Or place *tofu* in a flat-bottomed container and fill with water and cover. Keep *tofu* in the bottom of refrigerator. *Tofu* can be kept fresh for 3 to 4 days. If kept more than 3 to 4 days, it is recommended that *tofu* be boiled in salted water for 2 to 3 minutes. Do not freeze because the texture of *tofu* will change. However, if you prefer a different texture, you may try as follows: 1. Drain water from water-packed container. 2. Wrap *tofu* in plastic sheet. 3. Keep in freezer. 4. Color turns to light umber. This way frozen *tofu* can be stored indefinitely. Before cooking dip in water and remove plastic sheet and wash well. Frozen *tofu* has tender and meaty texture and makes excellent dishes with vegetables. To cook fresh *tofu*, do not overcook. Always add *tofu* last in cooking. Also for better cooking, drain water out before cooking. It gives a firmer and richer flavor. Keep *tofu* in refrigerator for a couple of hours or overnight. Or faster results, see illustration below. For faster results, place *tofu* on several layers of towels on cutting board and top with water-filled bowl. Change the towels often.

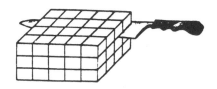

Cut *tofu* into cubes.

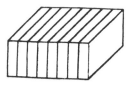

Cut *tofu* into ¹/₄-inch (0.7 cm) or ¹/₂-inch (1.5 cm) thick slices.

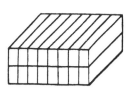

Cut *tofu* crosswise into halves; then slice into 8 pieces.

101

PREPARATION

Chicken Parts

a ······ Breast

b ······ Inner breast

c ······ Wings

d ······ Leg (Drumstick plus Thigh)

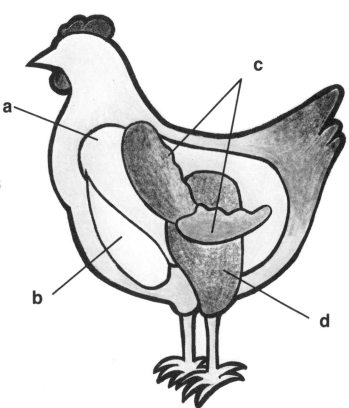

How To Make *Teriyaki* Sauce

Basic Sauce	Thick and Mild Sauce	Tomato Sauce Base Sauce

Makes 1/2 cup
 	
3 tablespoons sugar
3 tablespoons *sake*
3 tablespoons *mirin*
  or Japanese sweet cooking wine
3 tablespoons soy sauce
1 clove garlic, crushed
1-inch square ginger root, grated
	Makes about 1 cup
	
	1/3 cup *mirin*
	  or Japanese sweet cooking wine
	1/3 cup soy sauce
	1 1/2 to 2 tablespoons sugar
	1 teaspoon honey
		Makes 2 cups
		
		2 tablespoons chopped onion
		2 tablespoons chopped green pepper
		1 tablespoon vegetable oil
		1 can (8 ounces, 225 grams) tomato sauce
		1 tablespoon soy sauce
		1 tablespoon water
		1/4 cup rice vinegar
		1 tablespoon Worcestershire sauce
		2 tablespoons brown sugar
		1 tablespoon paprika
		1 teaspoon dry mustard
		1/2 teaspoon salt
		1/4 teaspoon chili powder
		1/8 teaspoon cayenne pepper

Lemon Flavored Sauce	**Mild Sauce**	**Hot-Spicy Sauce**

Makes 1/2 to 2/3 cup
 	
4 tablespoons olive oil
1-inch square ginger root, grated
1 clove garlic, crushed
1/2 teaspoon marjoram
1/4 teaspoon dried thyme
1/2 teaspoon grated lemon peel
1/4 cup lemon juice
1 tablespoon Chinese coriander
1 teaspoon paprika
1 teaspoon soy sauce
1/4 teaspoon salt
Dash of pepper
	For 2 large whole chicken breasts
	
	14 ounces (400 grams) red *miso*
	1/2 to 1 teaspoon Chinese chili paste
	1/4 cup *sake* or cooking wine
	1 teaspoon sugar
		Makes 2 cups
		
		4 tablespoons each red
		  and white *miso* (soy bean paste)
		1 clove garlic, crushed
		1/2 scallion, minced
		2 1/2 tablespoons sesame oil
		1/2 tablespoon chili pepper
		1 cup soy sauce
		2 tablespoons Kochu Jang (Hot Korean Sauce)
		1 teaspoon grated ginger juice
		1/4 medium apple, grated
		1/4 cup each *sake* and *mirin*
		  or Japanese sweet cooking wine
		2 1/2 tablespoons water
		6 tablespoons sugar

COOKING TIPS

Deep-frying

Tempura is a represented by "batter-fried" food in Japan. It is probably the best known Japanese dish.
    Four points for successful *Tempura*
1) Fresh ingredients.
2) Good vegetable oil.
3) Constant frying temperature.
4) Lumpy batter.
Prepare all ingredients to be deep-fried ahead of time. Preferably keep in a refrigerator until last minute. Make the *tempura* batter just before the actual deep-frying. The *tempura* batter, mixture of ice water, eggs and flour, should never be stirred well. Mix lightly — batter should be lumpy. All foods should be thoroughly dried before dredging. If you prefer a thick coating to thin batter, use less ice water than the recipe.
In general, deep-frying requires a large amount of oil in the wok, heavy cast iron skillet or deep-fryer. The use of polyunsaturated vegetable oil is strongly recommended for deep-frying. None of the pure vegetable oils contains cholesterol. The right temperature for deep-frying is 330–355°F (165–180°C). The oil should reach this temperature before any ingredients are added. An easy way to tell whether the oil has reached the desired temperature is adding a drop of batter into the oil. If the drop of batter reaches the bottom and slowly returns to the surface, the oil is not yet hot enough. If the batter drops half way to the bottom and immdediately bounces up to the surface, the oil is ready for deep-frying. Drop in ingredients and deep-fry until golden. Adjust the temperature to maintain a constant frying temperature. Frying temperature of 340°F (170°C) is recommended for vegetables. Use deep-frying thermometer to maintain a constant oil temperature. Skim the surface of the oil occasionally to keep it clean. Start with vegetables and then shrimp which requires a higher temperature. The oil used for deep-frying can be saved and reused. To grant your oil longer life, remove crumbs with a fine mesh strainer. The quality of used oil is judged by its clarity, not by the number of times used nor the length of time used. Fresh oil is light in color and clear. If the used oil is still relatively clear, it is readily usable again. For the second time round, it is recommended to deep-fry chicken or meats coated with bread crumbs. To remove odor in oil, deep-fry some potatoes uncoated. The moisture in potato absorbs odor while it is deep-fried. The proportion of 3:1 (used oil: fresh oil) is also usable again for deep-frying meats and chicken, but not for *tempura*. To store the used oil, first strain with a fine mesh strainer while oil is still hot. Then place the oil in a heatproof container and allow to cool. Cover and store in dark and cool place or in the refrigerator.

Grilling, Broiling, Pan-frying, Baking, Barbecueing

The grilling method is used to cook food quickly over very high heat so that the outside is crisp while the inside flesh remains tender and moist. The ingredients must be fresh. Grilling can be done with two different ways; direct and indirect heat. If you do charcoal grill, prepare charcoal fire in advance so that heat gets very hot. For stove top grilling, coat the rack with thin film of oil, then heat the unit before you place food on. Fish and meats are often marinated or basted with marinade sauces before and during cooking. Marinade sauces are combinations of *sake, mirin* or sugar, soy sauce and fresh ginger which has the same tenderizing enzyme as papaya and pineapple. Grill 60% on one side and 40% on the other side. For pan-frying, heat and add a small amount of oil. Heat the oil, then tilt the skillet so the oil covers the surface. When the oil begins to form a light haze, it is ready to pan-fry the ingredients. Cook over high heat, so that fish or meat except pork is tender and moist inside and the flavor is sealed in. If longer cooking is necessary, reduce heat and cover for a few minutes. You may need to add some marinade sauce to the pan. Then remove the lid and continue to cook until all liquid evaporates. For oven baking, preheat the oven to the required temperature and place food in the center of the oven to allow for even baking.

Nabemono Cooking (one-pot dishes)

Nabemono includes any dish that is cooked in one pot and eaten on the table. Therefore it has a great many varieties besides *sukiyaki* and *shabu-shabu*, and one of the main characteristics is in the cooking stock. In *sukiyaki* you only pick up solid ingredients from the pot, while in fish stew you take the broth together and enjoy it as a soup. In *shabu-shabu* or *mizutaki* or chicken hot pot you take the cooked but unseasoned ingredients and dip into sauces. In *oden-nabe* fish products and vegetables are stewed for a long time and eaten with the broth. In any type of *nabemono*, you can choose any ingredients you like. Basically *nabemono* needs no special cooking technique, but there are several points: When selecting ingredients, think not only of the colors but the affinity. Avoid harsh-tasting or strong-odor or fragile food. When preparing, cut each ingredient according to its cooking time so that all ingredients are ready to eat at the same time. Some foods need parboiling. *Daikon* radish and *konnyaku* must be parboiled to remove harsh taste. Dried foods should be softened well.

COOKING TIPS

Simmering

Simmering food requires special preparation for soup stock.

1) Simmering liquid is generally made of seasoned stock.
2) You may need some special cutting techniques for vegetables such as diagonal slices, flower-cuts, trimming to enhance the appearance of the finished dish.
3) Some ingredients need parboiling to remove harsh or bitter taste and rawness. Also, some ingredients take longer to cook. These ingredients are sometimes pre-cooked in different pans, then added to the simmering liquid.

   Simmered food can be served as a single dish or as one-pot dish. The ingredients and simmering liquid for the one-pot dishes are prepared ahead of time and arranged attractively on large platters.

The size of the pot is determined by the amount of ingredients to be cooked. A thick-bottomed pot will distribute the heat more evenly. If simmering for longer time, use a deep pot that holds an ample amount of simmering liquid. Slow electric cooker will have the same effect.

Use light seasoning for simmering liquid. The less the better. You can always add more later. In general add sugar or *mirin* first, then salt, rice vinegar (if recipe calls for) and soy sauce. Remember to control simmering temperature so that the liquid can be slowly absorbed into the ingredients.

Steaming

Steaming is one of the best way of retaining more nutrients and natural flavor than other conventional means of cooking. Steaming seals in the natural juices of meats and vegetables which are delicious when served over rice.

There are many different types of steamers. Wok with a cover will work as a good steamer. Multitiered bamboo steamers may be purchased. However, a large pot with a cover will suffice for the purpose of steaming food. Steaming racks are necessary to support and elevate the plate or bowl which holds food steamed in a wok. A round cake rack will do just as well as commercially available steaming racks. You may improvise water chestnut cans with both ends removed. The rack should be put in the center of the wok or pan.

All steamers operate according to the same basic principle. The efficient circulation of steam is of paramount importance. Bamboo steamers have several tiers in which many dishes can be steamed simultaneously. The tiers and cover are set on top of a wok containing boiling water. There are also metal steamers consisting of a pot to hold the water, usually two tiers and a cover. For example, the bottom pot cooks soup stock while the two tiers are used to steam two other separate dishes. In this manner, many dishes may be steamed at once saving time and energy.

Follow the steps below for effective steaming

1) Pour water into the wok or pot so that the water level stands one inch below the steaming rack or dish of food.
2) Cover the wok and bring the water to a full boil.
3) Use only heatproof dishes for steaming.
4) Place the dish of food atop the steaming rack. Cover and bring to the boiling point again. Turn the temperature down to medium high and allow to steam for the specified time.
5) Check the water level when longer steaming is necessary.

Stir frying, Sautéing

This cooking method combines the elements of high heat and constant tossing to seal in the flavor and juices of meat and vegetables. Thus, this technique is often used for Chinese cooking. Stir-frying cooks protein foods thoroughly at the same time leaving them tender and juicy. Vegetables retain their natural color and crisp texture when stir fried. It is important that slices are uniform in size so that they can be cooked evenly. Some vegetables may need parboiling before stir-frying. Prepare all necessary seasonings before stir-frying. Heat the wok or skillet until it barely gets hot and add a small amount of oil (usually 2 T), then roll the oil around to cover the surface of the wok. When the oil begins to form a light haze, add the ingredients. Follow the recipe and remember to adjust the temperature control at the proper stir-frying temperature. Actual stir-frying involves vigorous arm action in the constant stirring and tossing of the food. Serve immediately while still hot.

Timetable for Cooking Chicken

Cooking Method	Portion	Portion Weight ℓb: pound g: gram oz: once	Conventional Oven Temperature	Cooking Time h: hour min: minute	Internal Temperature
Roasting	Whole	2 to 2¹/₂ ℓb * [900 to 1175 g] 2¹/₂ to 3 ℓb [1175 to 1350 g] 3 to 4 ℓb [1350 to 1800 g] 4 to 6 ℓb [1800 to 2700 g]	325°F [165°C] 325°F [165°C] 325°F [165°C] 325°F [165°C]	1¹/₂ h. 2 h. 2¹/₂ h. 2¹/₂ to 3¹/₂ h.	180°F to 185°F [80°C to 85°C]
Baking	Broiler-fryer cut-up	3 ℓb [1350 g]	425°F [220°C]	45 min.	* Stuffed or unstuffed Ready-to-cook weight
Deep-Frying	Broiler-fryer cut-up	1¹/₂ to 2 ℓb [685 to 900 g]	[oil timperature] 375°F [190°C]	12 to 15 min.	
Grilling-Direct	Drumstick	5 to 6 oz [145 to 170 g]	Hot charcoal briquets	24 min.	
Grilling-Indirect	Whole	3 ℓb [1350 g]	Hot	70 min.	
Pan-Frying	Quartered fryer	2 to 2¹/₂ ℓb [900 to 1175 g]	Medium heat on top of range	60 to 75 min.	
Steaming	Breasts	2 large whole chicken breast	High heat on top of range	20 to 25 min.	
Stewing	Whole	3¹/₂ to 4 ℓb [1575 to 1800 g]	Medium to low heat	2 to 3 h.	
Stir-Frying	Wings or thighs	2 ℓb [900 g]	High to medium heat	20 to 25 min.	

General Rules for Chicken Cooked in the Microwave Oven

1. Six minutes to the pound on power level HIGH(9), full power.
2. Ten minutes per pound on power level Roast(7).
3. A broiler-fryer chicken will cook fast and it may requires a glaze, sauces or coating mixture to give extra color.

Cooking Whole Chicken in Microwave Oven

1. Cook whole chicken, uncovered, on a roasting rack.
2. Place the chicken, breast side down, with sauces in appropriate sized baking dish.
3. Cook for half of the estimated oven cooking time.
4. Drain off excess dripping if necessary. Turn chicken, breast side up, baste with drippings, or seasoned glaze.
5. Continue to cook, uncovered, for remaining time. If chicken wing tips and legs get brown, cover spots with small pieces of foil to prevent over cooking. Make certain that the foil does not touch the sides of the Microwave oven as it may pit them.
6. Food probe inserted in thickest part of thigh should read about 170°F (77°C) at the end of cooking time.
7. Remove from oven. Allow to stand 10 to 15 minutes. With foil tent.

Note: You can precook the chicken in minutes under microwave oven, then make it crispier over charcoal.

Cooking Chicken Pieces in Microwave Oven

1. Place chicken skin side down in shallow glass dish. Make sure the thicker portions are near the outside of dish, with the thinner portions nearer the center.
2. Cook, covered with wax paper, on HIGH power 6 to 7 minutes per pound or until throughly cooked.
3. If you prefer browning the chicken pieces, brown them first, then finish cooking in the microwave oven.
4. Sauces should be added at the beginning of cooking time.
5. Turn chicken pieces over halfway through cooking.
6. Allow to stand 5 to 10 minutes before serving.

UTENSILS

LACQUER WARE

For serving foods lacquer ware is used in Japanese cooking. New ones have some odor, so wipe them with vinegar, using lint free soft cloth. Leave it in well ventilated dark place. Do not use dish soap. Avoid prolonged soaking in hot or cold water. To retain beautiful glossy shine, dab on a bit of oil with cotton and wipe off thoroughly with a soft cloth. Be careful not to scratch them with finger nails or ring. To store wrap with tissue paper. Do not put in the dishwasher.

MEASURING UTENSILS

Measuring by the eye often causes waste of food or failure of seasoning. Be sure to measure in the right way.

[Kitchen Scales]
For home use, choose 5 lb/2 kg scales, with a large dish. Flat plate does not hold flour or nuts well. Do not leave things on the dish as it damages the spring.

[Measuring Cup]
1 cup is equivalent to 240 ml in this book. Usually made of glass, stainless or plastic. Stainless cups are most durable while glass ones are easy to read.

[Measuring Spoons]
There are four graduated sizes, tablespoon (T), teaspoon (t), half teaspoon ($1/2$ t), and quarter teaspoon ($1/4$ t). 1 tablespoon is equivalent to 15 ml or 3 teaspoons. 1 teaspoon equals 5 ml. To measure dry ingredients, scoop into appropriate spoon until full, and level with a spatula/knife.

MEAT POUNDER

Used to break down connective tissue of meat. It also level the thickness of meat, wrap and tap lightly with only this weight. It comes in metallic, wooden, and plastic forms.

METAL STRAINER

Ideal for straining dry and liquid ingredients and also useful for sifting small amount of dry ingredients.

MICROWAVE RANGE

For cooking foods speedily and cleanly. Without heating the utensils or oven, only the foods are heated. The food must contain moisture, and metal container or china with metal decorations are not suitable (metals cause sparks). Microwaves do a good job in thawing frozen meats or fish.

OVEN THERMOMETER

Success of baking lies in the accurate oven temperature, so it is a good investment.

NON-STICK MUFFIN PAN and COOKIE SHEET

It is made of rustproof alminum. Before using for the first time and after each use, wash in hot suds and dry. Pre-condition by rubbing in small amount of salad oil on surface.

ONION CHOPPER

This tool is useful for chopping onion or nuts into small pieces without a risk to fingers.

OVEN WARE

This baking dish is safe for oven and microwave use. It can go from freezer to oven and is dishwasher-safe.

ROLLING PIN

This is useful tool to make pastries or pasta. Some recipe calls for rolling the dough as thin as possible with floured stockinet-covered rolling pin.

PRESSURE COOKER

Cooking by superheated steam under pressure reduces cooking time to $1/4$–$1/5$ of what conventional pan takes.

VEGETABLE STEAMER

For steaming food successfully, advance preparation of steamer is just as important as assembling ingredients. The steamer is adjustable according to the amount of food and size of pot you use.

WOK

There are round-bottomed and flat-bottomed, or one-handled and two-handled types. For home use, round bottomed ones with side handles are recommended. Materials should be cast-iron since stainless scorches easily and Teflon-coats are easily scarred. Cast-iron woks are multi-purpose pots; stir-frying, deep-frying, simmering and steaming with bamboo steamer.

BAMBOO SKEWERS

For Japanese cooking, bamboo skewers are a very handy tool. They are not only used for many grilled dishes, but to test foods for doneness by pricking and also for cooking raw shrimp; to prevent curling while boiling. They come in various sizes.
Moisten bamboo skewers before skewering for grilling to prevent breaking or burning. Wash and store them or throw away after one or several uses. Bamboo is a versatile plant; for centuries it's been proven in the Orient. You can use bamboo for various things: houses, furniture, fences, cooking utensils and so on. Bamboo shoots is edible while bamboo leaf is used as a wrapper.

GARLIC PRESS

Used to crush garlic clove.

UTENSILS

DONABE (EARTHENWARE CASSEROLE)

The *donabe* is made from special clay and can be used directly over the flame. Conventional oven-proof-ware like stoneware can never be put on direct heat. However, the Japanese *donabe* can be used in an oven as well. It retains heat well and distributes heat evenly. These are great advantages when cooking at the table.

The *donabe* comes in small one-portion size: 7-inch (18 cm), in medium size: 10-inch (25 cm), in large sizes: 12-inch (30 cm). The lid of a *donabe* is always glazed inside and out. The inside of the body is glazed but not the outside. For first time use, fill it with water and a pinch of salt and boil over moderate heat for 5 minutes. Before putting it on a burner the unglazed outside must be completely dry and it should not be put empty on a flame. In case it cracks, cook gruel rice (*okayu*) in it. The small cracks will be sealed by gruel rice. Despite its heavy appearance, a *donabe* is very fragile, so knocks and bumps should be avoided. When putting in a dishwasher, be careful so that it will not jiggle against other pots and pans.

EGG CUTTER

It is a handy tool to slice or chop hard boiled egg.

IRON PLATE

An iron plate is placed on a direct heat and used to grill meats and vegetables. It maintains the heat very well and gives a sizzling sound, which creates the nice atmosphere. After each use, scrub in hot water and dry over heat; rub a dab of salad oil all over.

GRATER

Graters come in red copper, aluminum, pottery, stainless and plastic forms. Tin-plated copper graters will last longer. After each use, wash under running water to remove tissues between 'teeth' and scrape off tiny tissues using a toothpick. To prevent rusting, scrub in vinegar and salt mixture.

GREASE SKIMMER

This is used for taking grease out. Skim surface grease off of the soup, gravies or fried foods. After each use, pull back ferrule and rinse in hot running water or immerse in suds. Place in machine's utensil holder with fiber end up.

BAMBOO STEAMERS

For effective steaming, put on a wok filled with boiling water. Bamboo steamers can steam any ingredients and can be stacked in two or three layers to steam different foods at a time. Good things about bamboo steamers are that the mesh lid controls the steam and does not drip onto ingredients. Choose 12-inch (30 cm) in diameter steamer for a regular wok.

JAPANESE GRINDING BOWL and PESTLE

The Japanese grinding bowl is a pottery bowl serrated on the inside. It comes in various sizes. The pestle is made of wood and also comes in various lengths. To clean the bowl, use the tip of a bamboo skewer to loosen any hard bits that stick in the bowl's grooves. Wash with a stiff brush under running water.

BAMBOO or WOODEN SPATULA

This is used for tossing and mixing rice or ingredients. As it does not break up the rice grains, it is used for serving also. Moisten before use each time.

CAST-IRON POT and PAN

This is a round cast-iron pan used for cooking *sukiyaki*, and for one-pot dishes for cooking meat or fish with vegetables. A new cast-iron pan needs seasoning. Scrub it in water, then fill it with water until almost full and bring to the boil. Discard the boiling water. Repeat 2–3 times to remove the protective oil applied when manufactured. Dry thoroughly. Then heat $1/2$ cup used oil in the pan and sauté some vegetable scraps until all vegetables are tender. Discard the vegetable scraps. Fill pan with water and bring to the boil. Rinse and repeat. Dry thoroughly or over moderate heat and rub a dab of oil on the inside surface to prevent rusting. If rust appears, simply scrub clean and re-season. But, never scour your pot with coarse grained cleansers. An electric Teflon coated skillet or wok is a good substitute. They are especially suited for entertaining or cooking at the table.

AUTOMATIC RICE COOKER

Today rice is cooked daily in many households in an automatic electric or gas rice cooker. The automatic rice cooker is an appliance developed in the postwar period, cooks perfect rice. Put washed rice in the cooker, add water. There are measurment marks in the cooker for water and rice volume. Then cover and turn on. Automatic controls take over cooking, reducing heat at exact time, and also in some models, the rice is kept warm till needed. Cookers come in various sizes, from tiny ones holding only a few cups to large ones used in restaurants. Automatic rice cookers, either electric or gas can be obtained at oriental stores.

CHOPSTICKS

Come in various lengths and styles. China, Korea and Vietnam also use chopsticks and each country has different types of chopsticks. Traditional Japanese chopsticks are made of bamboo or cedar. These materials were used so that the fine surface of the pottery would not be scratched and also Japanese like the touch of wood rather than metal. Chopsticks are all-purpose handy utensils for oriental cooks. Use them to reach the bottom of deep pots, pans and bowls and to stir, beat, whisk, turn food and lift all sorts of food.

INGREDIENTS

BAMBOO SHOOTS —— Cream colored, cone shaped shoots of bamboo. Canned shoots are most common. Once opened, store covered with fresh water up to 2 weeks in the refrigerator. Change water once every 4 to 5 days.

BEAN SPROUTS —— Sprouts of the mung bean; about 2-inch (5 cm) long. Refrigerate sprouts covered with water. Keeps for one week. Change the water every 3 days.

CHINESE MUSTARD, DRIED —— Pungent powder. Mix 1 tablespoon dry powder to 1 tablespoon water for average proportion. Store dry powder on shelf indefinitely.

COCONUT MILK —— It is made by soaking grated fresh or dried coconut in water, squeezing out the liquid, and discarding the coconut pulp.

DAIKON RADISH —— *Daikon* radish is rich in vitamins, and its leaves contain much calcium. This radish is thought to aid digestion of oily foods. It is good for simmered dishes.

FISH SAUCE —— Fish sauce is made by aging salted fish in large stone jars and filtering off the liquid. It is indispensable to Thai cooking. This condiment is also used for Vietnamese, Philippines and Burma cooking.

FIVE SPICE POWDER —— Blend of five ground spices: Szechwan peppercorns, star anise, cinnamon, fennel and cloves. Keeps on shelf for several months.

EGGPLANTS —— Eggplants used here are the 6-inch (15 cm) variety that weigh approximately 10 oz (285 g) each, rather than the small Japanese eggplants that are on the average 4-inch (10 cm) long and weigh 2–3 oz (60–90 g) each. Because size varies with region and season, weights are included to offer a guideline. If using the small Japanese variety, substitute 3–4 eggplants in these recipes.

GINGER ROOT —— Ginger is a pungent, aromatic rootstalk of a genus Zingiber, tropical Asiatic and Polinesian herb. It is a popular spice all over the world. The pungent substance promotes both appetite and digestion. When using for stir-fried dishes, shred and cook in hot oil to extract the aroma. In this oil cook the other ingredients. Choose fresh root without wrinkles.

HOISIN SAUCE —— Pungent, sweet condiment sauce made of soybeans, spices, chili and sugar. Once opened, store in a jar with tight lid. Keeps refrigerated for about 6 months.

HOT BEAN PASTE (chili paste with soybeans) —— Soybean sauce made from soybeans, chili peppers and sometimes garlic. Comes in cans or jars. Refrigerated, keeps indefinitely in tightly sealed jars. Degree of hotness may vary between different brands.

JAPANESE CUCUMBER —— Recipes in this book call for American cucumbers, which are equivalerent to 2 or 3 Japanese cucumbers. In general, peel and seed cucumbers unless skin is delicate and thin and seeds are immature. If using the Japanese variety, it is not necessary to peel or seed. However to smooth the rough surface and to bring out the skin color, dredge the cucumber in salt and roll it back and forth on a cutting board using the palm of your hand. Wash well.

JAPANESE HOT PEPPER —— Red pepper is used fresh or dried. Dried and ground coarse pepper is called *ichimi*, or one flavor spice. This *ichimi* is one of the component ingredients of *shichimi* or 7-spice mixture. *Shichimi* is a collection of seven dried and ground flavors: red pepper flakes (*togarashi*); roughly ground, brown *sansho* pepper pods; minute flakes of dried mandarin orange peel; dark green *nori* seaweed bits; black hemp seeds; white poppy seeds; and black sesame seeds.

KAMABOKO · CHIKUWA (steamed fish paste) —— *Kamaboko* is made mainly from fish protein. Good *kamaboko* is white and elastic and the cut end is glossy. Keep in refrigerator. *Chikuwa* literally means ring of bamboo. Both *kamaboko* and *chikuwa* go well with horseradish soy sauce.

KOMBU (kelp) —— *Kombu* is one of the basic ingredients used for making *dashi* stock. When you use it, never wash or rinse. The speckled surface of the kelp holds flavor, so do not wash. Kelp contains the most iodine of all seaweeds.

INGREDIENTS

LEMON GRASS —— Fresh or dried form is available at Asian markets and is used in Thai cooking.

LOTUS ROOT —— The flesh is white and "crunchy". Long tubular hollows run through the entire length of the root. When preparing lotus root for cooking, pare it first. Then cut into rounds. The shape should be attractive. To prevent discoloring it should be immersed for a short time in a mixture of alum and water or vinegar and water. This also gets rid of any hashness in flavor. It can then be boiled in water containing a little vinegar. It goes well with vinegared dishes.

MIRIN —— *Mirin* is heavily sweetened *sake*, used for cooking. *Mirin* is called "sweet cooking rice wine". *Sake* sweetened with sugar can be substituted.

MISO —— *Miso* is fermented soybean paste. The colors range from yellow to brown; yellow *miso* is referred to as white *miso* in this book. Brown *miso* is called red *miso*. Since there are various kinds of *miso*, it might be helpful to learn about *miso* by buying small quantities of various kinds. It is used for soups, dressings, sauces, etc.

OYSTER SAUCE —— Thick brown sauce made from oysters and soy sauce. Used to enhance flavor or as a dip. Keeps indefinitely in the refrigerator.

PARSLEY, CHINESE (Coriander or cilantro) —— A leafy parsley with a pungent flavor. Use as a garnish. Also may be used to add flavor to most any dish.

SAKE —— *Sake* is made by inoculating steamed mold (*koji*) and then allowing fermentation to occur. It is then refined. In Japan, *sake* is the most popular beverage but it is also used in various ways in cooking.

SAUSAGE, CHINESE —— Cured pork sausages about 6-inch (15 cm) in length with a sweet flavor. Refrigerate up to one month or freeze up to several months.

SESAME SEED OIL —— Made from sesame seeds which are rich in oil and protein. This oil has a unique taste and aroma. It is mixed with salad oil and used for frying *tempura* or used to add flavor and aroma to the dressing used on Japanese-style *aemono* dishes.

SESAME SEEDS —— Both black and white sesame seeds are used in Japanese cooking. when toasted, sesame seeds have a much richer flavor. Still richer, however, are ground sesame seeds. To grind sesame seeds use a *suribachi* (Japanese grinding bowl). Before grinding, toast seeds in a dry frying pan. It is a nice garnish.

SHIITAKE MUSHROOMS —— Both fresh and dried *shiitake* mushrooms can be obtained. Dried ones should be soaked in water before using. This soaking water makes *dashi* stock (Japanese soup stock). Fresh *shiitake* mushrooms have a distinctive, appealing "woody-fruity" flavor. *Shiitake* mushrooms are good for simmered dishes because of their special flavor. The best one has thick, brown velvety cap and firm flesh.

SZECHWAN PEPPER CORNS —— Dried berry of the prickly ash. It is not hot but has a slow numbing effect. Toast lightly in fry pan; finely crush to a powder. Strain through a fine mesh strainer to filter coarse shell.

TONKATSU SAUCE —— Japanese prepared sauce used as a dip for a pork cutlet.

VINEGAR —— Japanese rice vinegar is milder than most Western vinegars. Lightness and relative sweetness are characteristics of rice vinegar. Use cider vinegar rather than anything synthetic if substituting.

WATER CHESTNUTS —— Walnut sized, brown bulb. Must be peeled before use. It is sweet and has a crisp texture similar to apples. Canned water chestnuts are peeled and boiled. They will keep covered with fresh water, in the refrigerator, for about 2 weeks. Change the water once a week.

WINE, SHAOHSING or RICE —— Chinese rice wine used for drinking or cooking. Dry sherry may be used as a substitute in cooking.

WINTER MELON —— A large light green melon with a white powdery surface resembling a water melon. The inside is white with seeds in the center. Usually sold in sections. Peel hard skin and discard seeds. Slice melon and use in soups.

YAM NOODLE (shirataki) —— Thin transparent gelatin-like noodles, similar to bean threads. It is made from devil's tongue root, has no calories. *Konnyaku* made from the same root.

METRIC TABLES

Today many areas of the world use the metric system and more will follow in the future. The following conversion tables are intented as a guide to help you.

General points of information that may prove valuable or of interest:
1 British fluid ounce = 28.5 ml
1 American fluid ounce = 29.5 ml

1 Japanese cup = 200 ml
1 British cup = 200 ml = 7 British fl oz
1 American cup = 240 ml = 8 American fl oz

1 British pint = 570 ml = 20 British fl oz
1 American pint = 470 ml = 16 American fl oz
T = tablespoon   oz = ounce   g = gram   ml = milliliter

Weights

ounces to grams*	grams to ounces
1/4 oz = 7 g	1 g = 0.035 oz
1/2 oz = 14 g	5 g = 1/6 oz
1 oz = 30 g	10 g = 1/3 oz
2 oz = 60 g	28 g ≒ 1 oz
4 oz = 115 g	100 g = 3 1/2 oz
6 oz = 170 g	200 g = 7 oz
8 oz = 225 g	500 g = 18 oz
16 oz = 450 g	1000 g = 35 oz

grams × 0.035 = ounces
ounces × 28.35 = grams

* Equivalent

Linear Measures

inches to centimeters	centimeters to inches*
1/2 in = 1.27 cm	1 cm = 3/8 in
1 in = 2.54 cm	2 cm = 3/4 in
2 in = 5.08 cm	3 cm = 1 1/8 in
4 in = 10.16 cm	4 cm = 1 1/2 in
5 in = 12.7 cm	5 cm = 2 in
10 in = 25.4 cm	10 cm = 4 in
15 in = 38.1 cm	15 cm = 5 3/4 in
20 in = 50.8 cm	20 cm = 8 in

inches × 2.54 = centimeters
centimeters × 0.39 = inches

in = inch   cm = centimeter

Temperature

Fahrenheit (F) to Celsius (C)		Celsius (C) to Fahrenheit (F)	
freezer storage	−10°F = − 23.3°C	freezer storage	−20°C = − 4°F
	0°F = −17.7°C		−10°C = 14°F
water freezes	32°F = 0 °C	water freezes	0°C = 32°F
	68°F = 20 °C		10°C = 50°F
	100°F = 37.7°C		50°C = 122°F
water boils	212°F = 100 °C	water boils	100°C = 212°F
	300°F = 148.8°C		150°C = 302°F
	400°F = 204.4°C		200°C = 392°F

The water boiling temperatu
given is at sea level.

Conversion factors:

$$C = \frac{(F - 32) \times 5}{9}$$

$$F = \frac{C \times 9}{5} + 32$$

C = Celsius   F = Fahrenheit

INDEX

◇NTC **NISHIMOTO TRADING CO., LTD.**

IMPORTERS AND EXPORTERS

HEAD OFFICE: 2–11 KAIGAN-DORI 3-CHOME, CHUO-KU, KOBE, 650 JAPAN
TEL: (078) 391–6911~9 TLX: 5623820 NTC KB J FAX: (078) 391–1058

TOKYO OFFICE: 2–14 SOTOKANDA 3-CHOME, CHIYODAKU, TOKYO, 101
JAPAN TEL: (03) 253–5220~6 TLX: 2225504 NTC TK J FAX: (03)
257–1698

NAHA OFFICE: 1–9, MATSUYAMA 1-CHOME, NAHA, OKINAWA, 900 JAPAN
TEL: (0988) 66–1136~8 FAX: (0988) 66–6212

NEW YORK OFFICE: 21–23 EMPIRE BLVD. SOUTH HACKENSACK. N.J. 07606
TEL: (201) 641–4300 (212) 349–0056 TLX: 126663 NISHIMOTO J CTY FAX:
(0011) (201) 646–9450

LOS ANGELS OFFICE: 2474 SOUTH MALT AVENUE LOS ANGELES, CALIF.
90040 TEL: (213) 889–4100 TLX: 67400 NISHIMOTO LSA FAX: (0011)
(213) 888–0586

SAN FRANCISCO OFFICE: 410 EAST GRAND AVENUE. SOUTH SAN FRAN-
CISCO, CALIF. 94080 TEL: (415) 871–2490 TLX: 278037 NISHI UR FAX:
(0011) (415) 588–5838

HONOLULU OFFICE: 537 KAAHHI STREET, HONOLULU, HAWAII 96817
TEL: (808) 847–1354 (808) 848–0761 TLX: 8478 NTC HR FAX: (0011) (808)
841–3853

DUSSELDORF OFFICE: BEETHOVENSTR 19, 4000 DUSSELDORF 1, WEST
GERMANY TEL: (0211) 660884 TLX: 8586453 NTCD D